Austin

A HISTORICAL PORTRAIT

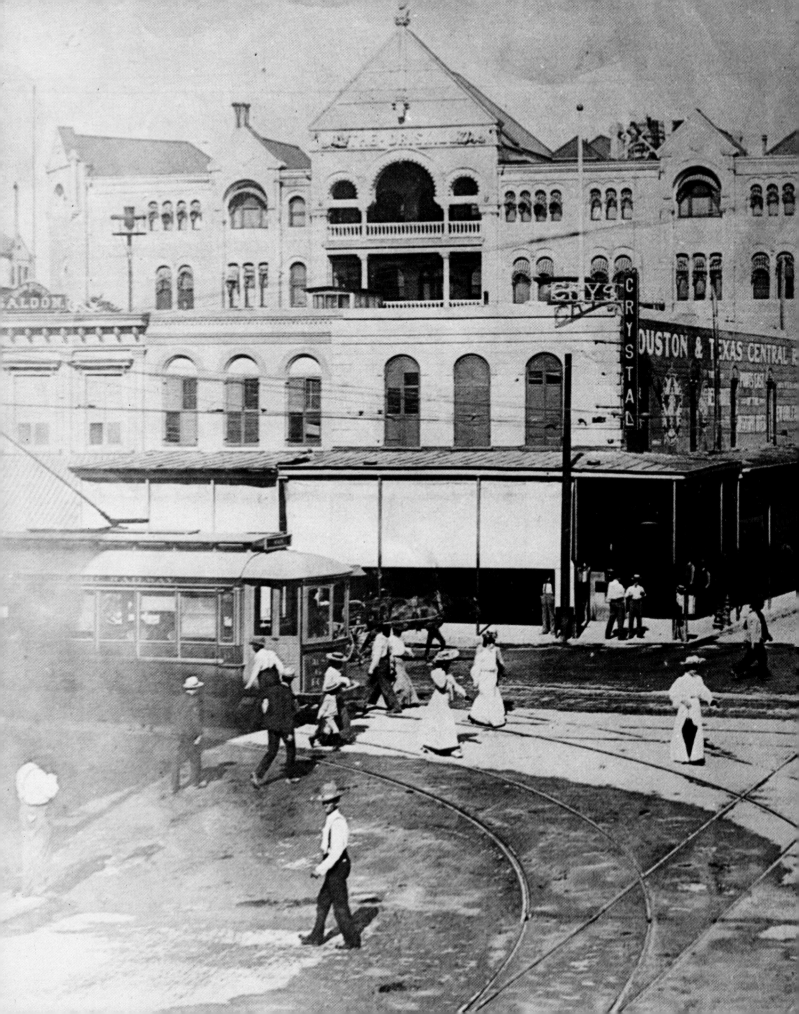

Austin

A HISTORICAL PORTRAIT

by Larry Willoughby

Design by Jamie Backus-Raynor
Donning Company/Publishers
Norfolk/Virginia Beach

The Donning Company/Publishers
5659 Virginia Beach Boulevard
Norfolk, Virginia 23502

Library of Congress Cataloging in Publication Data

Main entry under title:

Austin: a historical portrait

   Includes index.
    1. Austin, Tex.—Description—Views.
2. Austin, Tex.—History Pictorial works.
I. Willoughby, Larry.
F394.A943A86   976.4'31   80-22807
ISBN 0-89865-078-X   AACR1
Printed in the United States of America

4

Contents

Foreword

Most people who have lived in Austin for any length of time tend to agree that it is about the primest town in Texas. I have had such feelings about Austin ever since the stork dropped me off there sixty-seven years ago. My Cousin Ed, an elderly relative who used to live with us when I was a small boy, carried the pro-Austin sentiment even further than that. He had been born in Austin seventy-odd years earlier, and he boasted that he had never allowed himself to be tempted to travel further away from there than the Dallas Fair. And that was only once, in 1920.

"Once I realized the Lord intended Austin to be the center of the universe," Cousin Ed explained, "I never wanted to get far away."

When we would ask how he knew the Lord intended Austin to be the center of the universe, he would answer with irrefutable logic. "If God hadn't intended Austin to be the center of the universe, he wouldn't of went to the trouble of puttin' it thar!"

I've decided Cousin Ed had a point. Larry Willoughby relates an account in this excellent book of how the new government of the Republic of Texas sent out a commission in 1839 to locate a site for a new capital. The members of the commission reported that the site they chose, in addition to having a multitude of natural assets, was located as nearly in the middle of Texas as they could possibly put it! And that's where Austin has been ever since — deep in the physical and spiritual heart of Texas, if not the universe.

The many state government offices and the University of Texas have also made Austin the center of political and educational life in Texas and have lent a certain aura of enlightenment and excitement to life there. These factors, combined with natural charms and beauty, have given Austin unique qualities that have caught the fancy of the Cousin Eds and his like since its founding.

Today, however, with the hodge-podge of mindless development and the grotesque urban sprawl that keeps multiplying by the hour, Austin is fighting to hold its own. Those of us who still have strong emotional ties to the particular mystique that gave Austin its charm must view with distress the obliteration of so much that we cherished. In this book Larry Willoughby portrays that mystique and brings it to life. So enjoy this trip through Austin's past, and don't despair. After all, Barton Springs is still there!

— John Henry Faulk

Photo
ELLISON
-Austin-

Preface

In 1880 a Dallas newspaper ridiculed the Austin city government for passing anti-pollution ordinances intended to protect the Colorado River. The *Dallas Herald* editorial called the leaders of Austin "stupid and backward" and the citizens of Austin "want of enterprise." One hundred years later Austin in many ways is still out of step with other Texas cities. It is not uncommon today to hear criticisms of Austin's concern about uncontrolled growth, its progressive political climate, or the casual and open atmosphere that prevails in the city.

A tradition that has endured throughout the 142-year history of Austin transcends the usual claims of civic pride and boosterism. Austin has a progressive spirit that welcomes change and encourages diversity, yet it also cherishes the values and heritage of the past. Perhaps that overused and misunderstood phrase, quality of life, best describes the physical, intellectual, and spiritual environment which surrounds Austin and its citizens. Nowhere is the quality of life as rich as in Austin, Texas.

This book is not, of course, a comprehensive history of Austin or its citizenry. It is an attempt to portray pictorially the essence of Austin and its people throughout the last century and a half. Hopefully, it will stimulate and encourage more interest and more study into the lives and contributions of previous generations who built this unique city.

The major source of the pictures comprising this work was the Austin-Travis County Collection which is located in the Austin Public Library. Several of the pictures in this book have appeared previously in various library publications, but their quality and importance required that I include them. I would like to thank the staff of the Austin-Travis County Collection (Audray Bateman, Frances Moore, Kathleen Sykes, Sharmyn Lumsden, Karen Warren, Mary Jo Cooper, Linda Zezulka, Nancy Byrd, and May Schmidt) for their assistance, patience, and extensive knowledge. This project could not have been completed without their invaluable contributions.

The staff of the Barker Texas History Center at the University of Texas graciously assisted in my research efforts. I also thank Roger Griffin of Austin Community College for his help and suggestions. Special thanks go to Bobby Willoughby for correcting the manuscript and to Pauline Robertson for introducing me to this project. I thank Robyn Turner for her assistance and support.

I wish to acknowledge my appreciation to John Henry Faulk, a man whose spirit and strength have inspired me and who symbolizes what I feel Austin should represent.

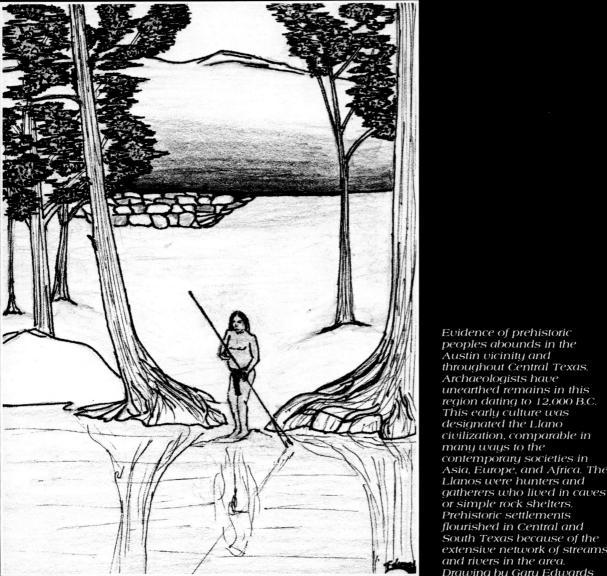

Evidence of prehistoric peoples abounds in the Austin vicinity and throughout Central Texas. Archaeologists have unearthed remains in this region dating to 12,000 B.C. This early culture was designated the Llano civilization, comparable in many ways to the contemporary societies in Asia, Europe, and Africa. The Llanos were hunters and gatherers who lived in caves or simple rock shelters. Prehistoric settlements flourished in Central and South Texas because of the extensive network of streams and rivers in the area. Drawing by Gary Edwards

Chapter 1

The Republic: 1839 ~ 1845

Ancestors of the Llano Man lived in rock shelters near McKinney Falls on Onion Creek, just southeast of Austin. Artifacts at the site indicate the rock shelter was inhabited from 500 A.D. to the late 1700s. The last prehistoric group to occupy the shelter was closely related to the Tonkawa Indian tribe. Their weapons and tools were made of stone, bone, and wood. Food consisted of available plants such as fruits, berries, or roots and animals such as fish, buffalo, birds, deer, skunks, and turtles. The simple, tranquil lifestyle of these native Americans remained relatively the same for thousands of years until the arrival of the Europeans. Drawing by Gary Edwards

On January 14, 1839, the Third Congress of the Republic of Texas passed a bill creating a commission to locate a site for a permanent capital of the young nation. The first section of the act specified that "said site shall be located at some point between the rivers Trinidad and Colorado, and above the Old San Antonio Road." The second section of the bill provided that the name of the new capital should be Austin, in honor of the father of Texas, Stephen Fuller Austin. President Mirabeau B. Lamar quickly signed the legislation, and he personally greeted the five commissioners as they left Houston to seek a new capital and to create a new city.

In their report to Lamar in April of 1839, the commissioners explained why they selected a small frontier village named Waterloo on the banks of the Colorado River. The commission report described Waterloo in terms of the central location, the healthful climate, the fine water, the abundant stone, the available timber, and the overwhelming beauty of the terrain. The commissioners and President Lamar envisioned a time when great thoroughfares would be established between Santa Fe and Galveston and between the Red River and Matamoros. These two routes of travel and commerce would intersect precisely at the site of Waterloo. The new capital was destined to be, as one of the commissioners so aptly phrased it, a city of "grandeur and magnificence."

In April of 1839, President Lamar appointed an agent to lay out the proposed new capital city and to begin construction of government buildings. The man selected by Lamar was Judge Edwin Waller, a well-respected veteran of the Texas Revolution. Immediately after his arrival in early May, Waller chose the site for the city and then divided this 640-acre tract into lots. The city was bounded on the south by the Colorado River and on the east and west, in Waller's terms, by "two beautiful streams of clear water." In the northern part of the town survey, Waller designated a section as the future Capitol Square. He labeled another elevated area farther to the north as College Hill. Waller envisioned a capitol complex adjoining a future university as the heart and backbone of this new city.

Judge Waller, with the aid of surveyor William Sandusky, set up construction camps at Durham's Spring alongside Waller Creek, located at present-day Sixth Street and Nueces. These camps housed approximately 200 workers, most of whom were unskilled and inexperienced. The hardships they endured were enormous. The summer heat was at its peak. Their sparse diet consisted primarily of dried beef and water. In addition to physical discomforts, the fear of Indian attack was an overriding concern. Comanche raids were common near the base construction camp, and news of a scalping was not rare in those first months.

President Lamar and the members of his cabinet arrived in Austin on October 17, 1839. A month later the first session of the Fourth Congress of the Republic of Texas met at the new capitol building at Hickory (Eighth) Street and Colorado. Austin was now officially a functioning national capital. However, one of the first resolutions introduced by the new Congress called for a change in the seat of government. Although the resolution was defeated,

Placido, Chief of the Tonkawas.
Courtesy of Austin-Travis County Collection, Austin Public Library

Two other Indian cultures were present in the Central Texas area during the early nineteenth century, the Lipan Apaches and the Comanches. The Comanches were the most persistent and the most terrifying adversaries faced by the early Texas settlers. As the influx of Americans grew and the herds of buffalo dwindled, the Apaches and Comanches migrated westward, and by 1875 the Indian presence in Texas had virtually disappeared. Pictured are two Comanche warriors. Courtesy of Austin-Travis County Collection, Austin Public Library

it indicated a precarious future for the young city.

Life on the American frontier demanded optimism, and Austin's first citizens possessed an abundance of that resource. By the spring of 1840, government buildings were bustling with activity, and businesses were rapidly opening to serve the needs of the expanding population. Two newspapers, the *City Gazette* and the *Sentinel,* began operations and served as watchdogs for the public interest. Real estate dominated the economic scene, with the average city lot selling for about $400. Pine was shipped in from Bastrop to fill those lots with houses and businesses. Two churches, a Baptist and a Presbyterian, were constructed as well as six gambling casinos. The first census, taken in 1840, listed a total of 856 inhabitants, 711 white and 145 slave. In little over a year the population had increased from about 10 to nearly 1,000. Despite the apparent progress and prosperity, events in 1841 and 1842 not only destroyed Austin's optimism but also threatened its very existence.

Since Austin lay on the western edge of the Texas frontier, Indian raids against life and property were common. The continuing Comanche threat made it unsafe for anyone to travel outside the city's general vicinity unless protected by armed escort. This point was made dramatically in 1841 when Travis County's first county judge, James Smith, was killed by a Comanche raiding party. Judge Smith crossed Shoal Creek to search for stray cattle and ventured too far west of Treaty Oak, the symbolic dividing line between Anglo and Indian territory. As the Indian uprisings grew more frequent and more severe, legislators from the more populous East Texas and Gulf Coast regions complained bitterly about the dangers surrounding Austin. Led by the hero of the Texas Revolution, Sam Houston, critics repeatedly demanded that the capital be removed to safer quarters.

When Mexican troops under General Vasquez marched into San Antonio in March of 1842, many residents of the Colorado River valley panicked and evacuated the area. Those expressing anti-Austin sentiment now exploited the fear of the Mexican forces as well as that of the Indians in order to demonstrate the inadequacies of Austin's defenses. Sam Houston was now president of the Republic, and the tide of events supported his claim that Austin was too far out on the frontier to be a suitable capital. Under the continuing threat of Mexican attack, President Houston ordered the seat of government transferred back to Houston, presumably to protect the government archives from capture or destruction. This led to the so-called Archive War, a non-violent confrontation in which Austin citizens refused to let Houston's representatives remove the archives. Even though the archives remained in Austin, Congress met at Washington-on-the-Brazos and at Houston for the next three years.

Following the removal of governmental operations in March of 1842, Austin experienced the low point in its young history. The population steadily declined, and the vacant houses and businesses created the image of a ghost town. The boom-town atmosphere that was prevalent just three years earlier was non-existent. With the continual threat of Indian and Mexican attack, there was little reason to believe that Austin would survive. But the struggling town, kept alive by a few determined citizens and a primitive barter economy, did survive. In July of 1845, the new president of the Republic of Texas, Anson Jones, convened a Constitutional Convention in Austin. This convention fulfilled the requirements for Texas to be admitted as the twenty-eighth state of the United States of America. The future of Austin was once again a bright one, now as a state capital rather than a national one.

The first settlement in Travis County was at Hornsby Bend, just a few miles east of Austin. Reuben and Sallie Hornsby made their home at a bend in the Colorado River in 1832. Hornsby had been part of the original surveying crew that had laid out Stephen F. Austin's Little Colony in 1830. Hornsby Bend became a familiar stopping place for all the settlers who later came to Waterloo. The Hornsby Cemetery still remains and is located six miles east of Austin on Webberville Road. Author photo

Mirabeau B. Lamar, who served the Republic of Texas as president from 1838 until 1841, was instrumental in the final selection of Waterloo as the site of the nation's capital. Lamar had visited the area in the autumn of 1838 and had hunted buffalo with one of the white settlers in the area, Jacob Harrell. Lamar and his entourage camped alongside the Colorado River at the mouth of Shoal Creek. Viewing the beauty of the river and the hills, Lamar is said to have remarked that this spot should be the seat of the future empire. Courtesy of Austin-Travis County Collection, Austin Public Library

Jesse Tannehill was another member of that Little Colony surveying crew. He received a 4,428-acre land grant in 1832 along the Colorado River (the area known today as the Govalle section of Austin). Seven years later Jesse and Jane Tannehill settled on their land that became known as Montopolis. This is a photo of the Tannehill home, which was constructed in 1839. Courtesy of Anne C. McAfee

Austin was named for Stephen Fuller Austin, often referred to as the Father of Texas. His father, Moses Austin, received a grant in 1821 from the Mexican government to settle 300 families in Texas. Moses died before he could fulfill his dream, so his son Stephen became the first man to bring American colonists into Texas. Despite innumerable hardships, Austin's colony between the Colorado and Brazos rivers grew in the 1820s to number over 10,000 American inhabitants. When Stephen F. Austin died in 1836, he had already begun to see the clash of American and Mexican cultures which he had strived to avoid. Courtesy of Austin-Travis County Collection, Austin Public Library

Treaty Oak, beneath whose branches Stephen F. Austin reportedly signed the first boundary line agreement between the Anglos and the Indians. The giant live oak tree, which is over 600 years old, was the site of numerous treaty signings and other ceremonial events during the early years of Texas' existence. Treaty Oak has been pronounced by the National Forest Service as the "most perfect specimen of a tree in North America." It is located on Baylor Street between Fifth and Sixth. Author photo

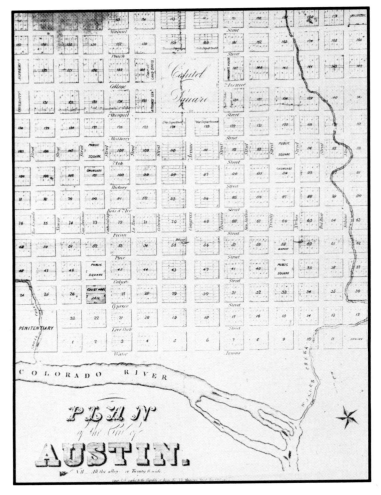

This plan of the city of Austin was the original layout completed by Judge Edwin Waller in 1839. The "two beautiful streams of clear water" that Waller intended to bound Austin were Shoal Creek on the west and Waller Creek on the east. The north-south streets were named for the rivers of the Republic. The east-west streets were named for trees common to Texas. In 1887 the east-west street names were changed to number designations. Courtesy of Austin-Travis County Collection, Austin Public Library

This drawing of the first Capitol building in Austin shows the Lone Star flag flying in 1839. The Capitol was located on the corner of Hickory (Eighth) and Colorado streets. Later a stockade was built surrounding the structure to protect it from Comanche or Mexican raids. Courtesy of Austin-Travis County Collection, Austin Public Library

William (Big Foot) Wallace was early Austin's most legendary and colorful figure. Big Foot was a Texas Ranger who gained fame as a fighter of both the Indians and the Mexicans. As an elderly Austin resident, Big Foot often reminisced of the days when he chased buffalo down Congress Avenue. Courtesy of Barker Texas History Center, University of Texas at Austin

Offices of the government of the Republic of Texas were housed in these three small frame buildings located just down the hill from the Capitol. The building on the left is the Department of the Navy. The center building is the Executive Department, and on the right is the Department of State. Courtesy of Austin-Travis County Collection, Austin Public Library

One of the first European countries to recognize Texas as a sovereign nation was France. The French Ambassador to Texas, Alphonse Dubois de Saligny, built this embassy in 1841 on Robertson Hill overlooking the city. The French Legation at 802 San Marcos Street has been restored and is now administered by the Daughters of the Republic of Texas. Courtesy of Austin-Travis County Collection, Austin Public Library

Travis County was named for the commander of the Texas forces at the Alamo, William Barret Travis. The Texas Congress designated the area surrounding Austin, previously part of Bastrop County, as Travis County on January 25, 1840. Courtesy of Austin-Travis County Collection, Austin Public Library

The Bullock Hotel was the scene of a celebration on October 17, 1839, to welcome President Lamar to Austin. Hosts at the dinner honoring Lamar were two of the Republic's most prominent citizens, General Albert Sidney Johnston and General Edward Burleson. The City Gazette reported that the celebration lasted from 3 until 8 p.m., with dinner repeatedly interrupted by toast after toast. For years the "loafer's log" in front of Bullock's was a favorite meeting place and relaxation spot. The Bullock Hotel was located at the northwest corner of Congress and Pecan (Sixth) streets. Courtesy of Austin-Travis County Collection, Austin Public Library

The mountaintop along the Colorado River was the most visible landmark to people entering the Austin vicinity. It was named Mount Bonnell, after early settler George Bonnell, a famous Indian fighter who became Commissioner of Indian Affairs for the Republic in 1838. A member of the ill-fated Santa Fe Expedition, Bonnell was killed in 1842 by Mexican soldiers on the Rio Grande River.

Just below Mount Bonnell on the river, a Mormon settlement was formed in the 1840s. The Mormons built a grist mill and a jail in Austin before a flood wiped out their entire community. Most of the original group moved on, settling near Burnet.
Courtesy of Austin-Travis County Collection, Austin Public Library

This artist's sketch depicts Austin as it appeared in 1844. Congress Avenue was the focal point of most activities and most commercial enterprises. Anyone who ventured west of Shoal Creek or south of the Colorado River did so at the risk of encountering unfriendly Comanches.
Courtesy of Austin-Travis County Collection, Austin Public Library

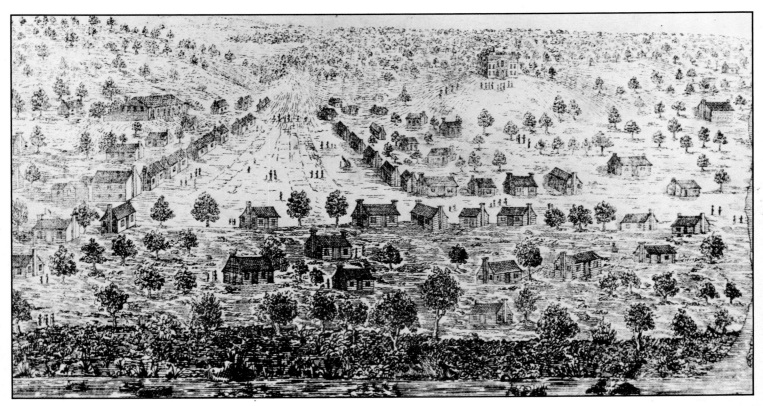

Chapter 2

The Lone Star State:

1845 ~ 1861

The foundation was laid for the old Capitol building in the spring of 1852. Newly inaugurated Governor Elisha M. Pease and the fifth legislature of Texas began conducting state business there in December of 1853. Courtesy of Austin-Travis County Collection, Austin Public Library

NEG.N⁰C·16

Statehood brought to Austin an air of stability and a sense of security. The promise of federal troops to guard the frontier against hostile Indians reassured Austinites and silenced many critics who questioned Austin's fitness to be a capital city. With J. Pinckney Henderson's inauguration as Texas' first governor and the convening of the first state legislature in 1846, Austin's future as the permanent capital appeared secure.

Soon after annexation to the United States, immigrants from other states and other countries began pouring into Texas and Austin. The population of the capital city rose rapidly, confronting its citizenry with new and larger problems. Despite its apparent rebirth, Austin was still a frontier settlement. Its remote location made difficult the transport of supplies to or from the ports along the Gulf Coast. Heavy rains sometimes made trips overland by wagon or stage nearly impossible. Although this lack of a satisfactory transportation system adversely affected all commercial ventures, it affected area farmers most severely, for they had no means to ship their surplus agricultural products to market. To combat this problem, enterprising residents of Austin saw the Colorado River as the answer to the transportation dilemma.

Although small rafts and flatboats routinely navigated the Colorado, no steamboat reached Austin until 1846. Following that momentous event, several attempts were made in the 1840s and 1850s to open a successful steamboat line along the river. Steamboats such as the *Kate Ward* and the *Colorado Ranger* made gallant efforts to serve the Colorado, but the shallow river was too slow and hazardous. By the eve of the Civil War, all efforts to establish a regular steamboat route had been abandoned.

Austin, however, did have many successful ventures during this period in its history. Businesses of every description appeared on Congress Avenue and Pecan (Sixth) Street. Austin had two weekly newspapers, the *Texas State Gazette* and the *Southwest American*. United States postal service routes came to Austin and the surrounding villages in 1849. Roads were modernized throughout Travis County, and two ferry companies operated on the Colorado River. Private academies and parochial schools opened to meet the educational needs of Austin young people. As the city grew more populous and more prosperous, its residents began to demand the culture and comfort that their fellow Americans to the east enjoyed.

The most notable aspect of Austin life in the 1850s was the building boom. Log cabins and lean-to offices were replaced by classic colonial houses and permanent brick buildings. The winter of 1853 saw the completion of the new Capitol building, located at the head of Congress Avenue in the spot reserved by Judge Waller as Capitol Square. The Governor's Mansion was constructed at its present site in the classic Greek-revival style representative of the antebellum South. Work on the Land Office Building was begun in 1856. Plans were devised for the state asylums, the state library, the treasury building, and other government offices.

The building fever also infected the church groups which were an integral part of Austin's social life. The Methodist Church at Congress and Pine (Fifth) Street was the first church structure in town. The Presbyterians soon followed with a frame structure of their own. At the end of the 1850s the First Baptist Church, St. Mary's Cathedral, and St. David's Episcopal Church were

The only way to cross the Colorado River was by ferry. This photo of the Sam Stone Ferry was taken during the 1850s. Stone's Ferry operated from a landing at the mouth of Waller Creek. Just below Congress Avenue, another ferry was run by James Swisher. There was little competition, however, since the rates were set by the county. Courtesy of Austin-Travis County Collection, Austin Public Library

One of the first photographs taken in Austin captures the view west of Congress Avenue. The corner in the foreground is the southwest corner of Pine (Fifth) Street and Congress. The First Presbyterian Church is pictured in the upper right portion of the photo. That church building was built in 1851 and was located at Lavaca and Bois d'Arc (Seventh) streets. Courtesy of Barker Texas History Center, University of Texas at Austin

fully established with permanent buildings. The churches and the government buildings stood as the most important historical and architectural landmarks in nineteenth-century Austin.

The 1850s in Austin have been described as the "era of elegance," referring to the magnificent houses built during this period. Several master builders and craftsmen resided here by this time, Abner H. Cook being the most famous. The distinguished homes designed and constructed in the pre-Civil War era rival any built in Austin before or since, and the Greek-revival building tradition of the 1850s was one of the greatest legacies that the early Austinites left to later generations.

In 1856 the Austin population had surpassed the 3,000 mark. An informal census of that year revealed "4 artists, 29 clerks, 14 doctors, 35 lawyers, 119 mechanics, 34 merchants, 32 laborers, 13 traders, 18 teachers, 9 tavern keepers, and 1 gentleman." Although Austin had a high percentage of professional people among its population, it also had a substantial number of what were referred to as "drunken idlers." The number and variety of taverns along Congress Avenue and Pecan (Sixth) Street give some credence to that charge. However, the taverns were also filled with politicians, and politics made Austin tick.

The major political issue of the 1850s revolved around the debate over the extension of slavery into the western territories. Rhetoric poured from the editorial columns of the *Texas State Gazette* condemning those who advocated the abolition of slavery and chastising those who warned of impending disaster. Although there was just a handful of true abolitionists in Austin, by the end of the decade there were a great many Austinites who balked at the mention of secession to preserve the "peculiar institution" of slavery. But Texas was a Southern state, and the Southern point of view prevailed and increased in fervor.

As the political debates grew more heated, so did the Texas weather. Droughts in 1856 and 1857 created a devastating crop failure. Coupled with the national financial panic of 1857, the agricultural crisis brought a depression to the Austin economy. Austinites endured the economic hardships for over two years. There was little money in circulation, and people subsisted on short supplies of beef and bread. The hopes that had characterized the early years of the decade were tempered by harsh economic realities. But the rains finally came, and with them the fragile economy began an upward climb. Just as the crisis passed, a new and larger crisis emerged to confront not only Austin and Texas but also the entire nation.

St. Patrick's Church was constructed in 1852 at the corner of Brazos and Ash (Ninth) streets. The name of the church was changed in 1866 to St. Mary's Cathedral at the insistence of the German parishioners. St. Mary's is still located in the original location in downtown Austin. Courtesy of Austin-Travis County Collection, Austin Public Library

The Governor's Mansion, built in 1855, is located at Eleventh Street and Colorado. Courtesy of Barker Texas History Center, University of Texas at Austin

Constructed in the 1850s, the Old Land Office Building is still standing at its original site at Brazos and Mesquite (Eleventh) streets. The Land Office was designed and built by German architect Conrad Stremme, and the style of nineteenth century Germany is in contrast to the more popular Greek-revival trend in Austin at that time. The Old Land Office Building now is the home of the Daughters of the Confederacy and the Daughters of the Republic Museum. Courtesy of Austin-Travis County Collection, Austin Public Library

Inadequate fire protection was a major problem that confronted all towns on the frontier. Austin's volunteer firefighters were plagued by lack of supplies, finances, manpower, and water during their early years. It was 1858 before Austin's first fire company was officially organized. Courtesy of Henry Seekatz

One of Austin's earliest and most distinguished residents was the Swedish settler Swante Palm. A successful businessman, he encouraged other Swedish immigrants to settle here. Palm School was named for him in 1892. Before his death he donated his entire collection of rare books and manuscripts to the University. Courtesy of Austin-Travis County Collection, Austin Public Library

Woodlawn was originally built for James Shaw in 1853 by Abner Cook. Governor Elisha M. Pease bought the house in 1859, and his descendants lived there for over 100 years. It is now the residence of former Governor Allan Shivers. Courtesy of Austin-Travis County Collection, Austin Public Library

Colorado at Hickory (Eighth) Street was the site of the old City Hall and Markethouse, built by Abner H. Cook. At one time the jail was housed on its top floor. Courtesy of Austin-Travis County Collection, Austin Public Library

Built in 1854, the City Hotel was located at Congress Avenue and Pine (Fifth) streets. Courtesy of Austin-Travis County Collection, Austin Public Library

One of the early recreation spots in Austin was Seiders Spring, which was settled in the 1850s by Edwin Seiders and became a favorite swimming and picnic area. Later, Lee Edward Seiders installed bath houses and a dance pavilion. Seiders Spring remains a beautiful setting located at Thirty-Fourth Street and Shoal Creek.

General Custer stationed his troops at Seiders Spring in 1865. It is also believed that Robert E. Lee stayed there when he visited Austin. Courtesy of Austin-Travis County Collection, Austin Public Library

Austin's General Store was located at the corner of Colorado and Pine (Fifth) streets. R. Bertram and Company sold everything from farm supplies to ladies' corsets. Courtesy of Austin-Travis County Collection, Austin Public Library

Frontier children were taught self-defense and survival at an early age. Courtesy of Austin-Travis County Collection, Austin Public Library

Charles Johnson built this house in 1858 near Deep Eddy. Johnson, a Swedish immigrant, settled in Austin in 1854 and built a floating grist mill at Shoal Creek on the Colorado. He engaged in various occupations including cattleman, freighter, and homebuilder. Today the Johnson home at 2201 West First is headquarters for the American Legion. Author photo

In 1857 Edward Tips opened a hardware store on Congress Avenue. He was joined by his brother Walter in 1872, and the Tips Hardware Company grew to be one of Austin's most prosperous enterprises. Descendants of the Tips family operate the business to this day.

Walter Tips was not only a successful businessman; his civic contributions to Austin were numerous. Walter Tips was Austin's most admired and respected citizen at the turn of the century. Courtesy of Austin-Travis County Collection, Austin Public Library

Sam Houston, Texas' most famous citizen, is a genuine folk hero. Houston commanded the revolutionary army that won Texas independence, served as president of the Republic of Texas, was one of Texas' first United States Senators, and also served as governor of Texas. A pro-Union supporter, he fervently tried to dilute secessionist sentiment while governor. When he refused to take the pledge of allegiance to the Confederate Constitution, Houston was removed from office on March 21, 1861. *Courtesy of Austin-Travis County Collection, Austin Public Library*

Chapter 3

Civil War and Reconstruction: 1861 - 1877

Andrew J. Hamilton served Texas as governor and attorney general. Hamilton was best known as the leader of pro-Union forces in Austin before the Civil War. Appointed governor in 1865, Hamilton served his term when Texas was under the control of military authority. He ran for governor in 1869 on the Conservative ticket but lost to Edmund Davis by less than 1,000 votes in a controversial election. *Courtesy of Austin-Travis County Collection, Austin Public Library*

Only seven men voted against secession at the convention in 1861. They were regarded as traitors by most Texans. An Austin photographer who supported them took this picture just after the secession vote, but the picture was not printed or shown until sixty-six years later.

Left to right, top row: A.P. Shuford, James W. Throckmorton, Lemuel H. Williams, Joshua Johnson; bottom row: William H. Johnson, George W. Wright, Thomas P. Hughes. *Courtesy of Austin-Travis County Collection, Austin Public Library*

Nothing is so tragic as a civil war, countrymen fighting countrymen. The American tragedy of the 1860s touched Austin in a unique manner. Pro-Union sentiment ran especially high in the capital city, and the impending crisis divided both friends and families. Many of Austin's most prominent citizens were leaders of Unionist thought and activity before and during the war. No matter what their stand on slavery, and the vast majority of them supported it, these people believed the Union must be preserved; therefore, they opposed the secessionist movement aggressively. The largest pro-Union meeting in Texas was held in Austin in 1859 under the leadership of Austinites E.M. Pease, George Paschal, and A.J. Hamilton. Their objectives were to diffuse secessionist rhetoric and to support the presidential candidate who could best hold the Union together.

The slave population in Travis County had grown from 791 in 1850 to 3,136 by 1860. Even though the majority of slaves was owned by a minority of the population, Austinites were convinced that the slave system had become an integral part of the local economy. The secessionists felt a Republican president would endanger their economic interests and would challenge their concept of states' rights. Presidential politics was on everyone's mind, and the election of 1860 was the key to Austin's as well as the nation's future.

The candidate of the Southern wing of the Democratic Party, John C. Breckenridge of Kentucky, carried Travis County and Texas in 1860. After the news arrived that Abraham Lincoln was victorious, uncertainty and confusion dominated the mood of the Texas capital. Austinites gathered along Congress Avenue and discussed, argued, shouted, and sometimes fought. The "fire-eaters" wanted to secede. The "submissionists" wanted to accept Lincoln and hope for the best. Many wanted to return to the days of the Republic and ignore both factions. Sam Houston, who was governor at this time, was an avowed Unionist. He pleaded with the people to remain calm and to protest through legal means.

In January of 1861, a secession convention met in Austin and officially drew up an Ordinance of Secession. A month later, the people of Texas overwhelmingly voted to withdraw from the Union by a margin of over three to one. The vote in Travis County, however, was convincingly against secession, 704 opposed and 450 for. Pro-Union sentiment in Austin and Travis County was well known throughout the state, resulting in much bitterness and ridicule. Austin resident Amelia Barr reflected the views of many Texans when she commented, "I am ashamed to say that Austin is a scandalously Yankeefied Union-loving town, which means that the majority of citizens want peace...at any price."

After the war began, pro-Union forces were silenced. Preparations for the four bitter years of struggle could be witnessed throughout Austin. Local fighting units such as the Travis Rifles and the Tom Green Rifles were organized. Many of Austin's volunteers joined Terry's Texas Rangers, one of the Confederacy's most famous and most fearless military companies. Throughout the war years, Confederate troops camped along Shoal Creek, at Barton Springs, and on the Capitol grounds. Civilians were also doing their part in the war effort. Women in Austin organized the Soldiers Aid Society and the Ladies Needle Battalion. Businessmen donated finished goods and

General Albert Sidney Johnston was an Austin citizen who served as United States paymaster until 1854. Jefferson Davis once referred to Johnston as the Confederacy's finest military officer. Johnston's gravesite at the State Cemetery is marked by an ornate sculpture by Austin resident Elisabet Ney. Courtesy of Austin-Travis County Collection, Austin Public Library

supplies to support the Confederate army. Farmers contributed food and cotton. West of Austin, Thomas Anderson operated a mill which helped keep the Rebels supplied with gunpowder.

Unlike many Southern cities during the Civil War, Austin has no history of military battles or strategic fortifications. There were rumors of a Yankee spy network operating in the hills west of town, but there is no proof that these "Mountain Rangers" were more than a few disgruntled Union sympathizers. The Austin soldiers did their fighting in faraway places like Shiloh, Vicksburg, and Chancellorsville. They joined some 60,000 other Texans who served in the Army of the Confederacy, and many of them were among the half-a-million Americans who died in the conflict.

The Reconstruction period in Austin was not as lengthy nor as restrictive as in many Confederate capitals. Military rule, originating from the Fifth District headquarters in New Orleans, was in effect for only a brief period. No Texans were imprisoned or punished for their Confederate loyalties. No Texan's land or property was confiscated. Basically, Texans ran the government during Reconstruction. The only requirement for readmission to the Union was a new constitution that prohibited slavery and accorded the freedmen their civil rights. The concept of a harsh and tragic Reconstruction period for Texans and Austinites was a myth.

Reconstruction for Black Austinites was a bittersweet experience. Resentment and animosity greeted most freedmen as they tried to enter the political and economic life of the community. By 1870, a local chapter of the Ku Klux Klan was enforcing its will through threat and intimidation. Despite such obstacles, freedom was now a reality, and black citizens were determined to achieve their full measure of it. The Reconstruction government created the Freedmen's Bureau and Union Leagues to aid and protect the Black population. For a few brief years, under the protective guidance of the Radical Republicans in Washington, Blacks did possess some semblance of political and civil rights.

Three areas in Austin became centers of Black settlement: Robertson Hill, Wheatville, and Clarksville. The majority of Black Austinites congregated east of East Avenue (near Robertson Hill) and on small tenant farms along the river. There was a Black community and school just west of San Gabriel and Orange (Twenty-Fourth) streets, named Wheatville. In 1871, ex-slave Charles Clark purchased a homestead west of Shoal Creek. This small enclave, called Clarksville, flourished in West Austin despite numerous attempts to destroy its unique cultural heritage.

As the war faded from memory, Austin and the entire nation entered a period of growth and prosperity. In a dynamic twenty-five year span, technology transformed the small frontier village of Austin into a modern capital city.

Anderson's Mill is located about eighteen miles northwest of Austin just a few feet from the shore of Lake Travis. This view of the mill in the 1860s shows Cypress Creek as it flowed toward the Colorado River.

Thomas Anderson used his mill during the Civil War to manufacture gunpowder. Pro-Union supporters tried to sabotage Anderson's Mill numerous times, but it continued to supply the Confederacy with powder throughout the war. Courtesy of Austin-Travis County Collection, Austin Public Library

Many Austin soldiers were members of Hood's Brigade. They fought in the western sector during the early stages of the war, but near the end they fought at the side of General Hood to protect Atlanta. Courtesy of Austin-Travis County Collection, Austin Public Library

General John B. Hood of Austin and Central Texas was one of the Confederacy's leading military figures. The world's largest military installation, Fort Hood, named after the general, is located sixty miles north of Austin. Courtesy of Austin-Travis County Collection, Austin Public Library

Confederate soldier John Pickle of Austin was a survivor of our country's greatest tragedy. Over 600,000 young men from both North and South were not so fortunate. Courtesy of Austin-Travis County Collection, Austin Public Library

Posing on the steps of the Confederate Veterans Home are six former members of Terry's Texas Rangers, who were among the Confederacy's most famous fighting units. Led by Benjamin F. Terry, the Rangers were also known as the Eighth Texas Cavalry. They originally numbered over 1,000 men, but by the war's end, only 300 were still alive. Courtesy of Austin-Travis County Collection, Austin Public Library

Following the Civil War, General George Custer and his troops were stationed in Austin. Custer's troops camped at various spots along Shoal Creek from Pease Park up to Seider's Springs. The general's military headquarters were at the Blind Asylum, which later became the Little Campus area at the University. This 1865 photo at the asylum pictures General and Mrs. Custer sitting on the porch. Courtesy of Austin-Travis County Collection, Austin Public Library

One of the "carpetbaggers" who came to Austin after the war was William Alexander, who arrived in 1866 and built his home, the Shot Tower, at 115 West Hickory (West Eighth). Rumors abounded about Alexander and his followers in those days of suspicion and mistrust. Republicans, freedmen, and other Yankee sympathizers reportedly met at the Shot Tower secretly to plot against those who still retained Confederate loyalties. The Shot Tower was demolished in 1974. Courtesy of Austin-Travis County Collection, Austin Public Library

In 1866 August Scholz, a German immigrant and Confederate veteran, opened a beer garden on San Jacinto Street. Legislators, college students, and business people have socialized at Scholz Garden since that time and have made it one of Austin's most famous landmarks. Pictured is T.A. Reisner. Courtesy of Austin-Travis County Collection, Austin Public Library

Since cotton was a major cash crop in the farm belt east of Austin, slave labor was employed to work the fields. However, the slave system was never as integral a part of the Austin economy as it had become in other parts of the Cotton Kingdom. Courtesy of Austin-Travis County Collection, Austin Public Library

Black Texans did not receive word of their freedom until well after the war was over, June 19, 1865. Since that time, the Black community in Texas has celebrated the event by observing "Juneteenth." These Austin citizens, donned in their Sunday finest, have gathered in Pease Park to celebrate Emancipation Day. Courtesy of Austin-Travis County Collection, Austin Public Library

The Cotton Exchange was an important factor in the economy of Travis County during the nineteenth century. Even after the slaves were freed from the cotton fields by the Civil War, cotton continued to be the main cash crop in the area. Courtesy of Barker Texas History Center, University of Texas at Austin

This log cabin was part of the old slave quarters of a cotton farm located near Oak Hill. The Oak Hill community, just a few miles southwest of Austin, was originally called Oatmanville. Later it was named Shiloh and Live Oak before settling on its present designation. Courtesy of Austin-Travis County Collection, Austin Public Library

Much of the strength of the Black community came from their religious heritage. This nineteenth century photo pictures the choir from the Sweethome Baptist Church. Sweethome has been the social center of the Clarksville area in West Austin since its inception in the early 1880s. Courtesy of Clarksville Neighborhood Center

One of the early families to settle in the Clarksville area was the Williamson family. Courtesy of Clarksville Neighborhood Center

Five young men who grew up in Clarksville, the Bolden brothers. Courtesy of Clarksville Neighborhood Center

Business activity did not venture far from Congress Avenue in the 1860s. Only a few buildings can be seen in this view up Bois d'Arc (Seventh) Street toward the east. The clock atop B.C. Wells' Jewelry Shop was a landmark in this part of town for many years. Courtesy of Austin-Travis County Collection, Austin Public Library

It appears as if the entire population of Austin turned out in May of 1867 to watch John Devier walk across Congress Avenue on a tightrope. Governor Pease, whose carriage is on the left, was one of the spectators enjoying the exciting event. Courtesy of Austin-Travis County Collection, Austin Public Library

Dr. Samuel G. Haynie, having arrived in 1839, was one of Austin's first doctors. This 1860s picture shows his office and drug store, located on the 800 block of Congress Avenue. Dr. Haynie served Austin as postmaster, councilman, and congressman. Courtesy of Austin-Travis County Collection, Austin Public Library

"No women allowed" was the greeting on the sign at the San Antonio Saloon. Not all Austin taverns barred women, but drinking in public and the consequences that often resulted were considered strictly in the masculine domain. Courtesy of Barker Texas History Center, University of Texas at Austin

Photographs of Austin were rare before the 1860s. This Congress Avenue scene features one of Austin's first photography studios, the gallery of H.B. Hillyer. Courtesy of Austin-Travis County Collection, Austin Public Library

Hillyer Photography received most of its competition from William Oliphant. Oliphant's Gallery was a showcase for the newest in portrait photography as well as an art gallery for local artists. Courtesy of Austin-Travis County Collection, Austin Public Library

By 1869 a pontoon bridge was constructed across the Colorado River at the foot of Congress Avenue. However, a flood the following year washed it away, so once again the only way to cross the river was by ferry. *Courtesy of Austin-Travis County Collection, Austin Public Library*

The railroad finally reached Austin in 1871. The Houston and Texas Central Railroad had extended its lines to Bastrop by the late 1850s, but the Civil War delayed the thirty-mile move westward. This is a photo of the H.&T.C. depot at Congress and Cypress (Third) Street. *Courtesy of Austin-Travis County Collection, Austin Public Library*

After the railroad arrived in 1871, the stagecoach soon became obsolete. The General Sam Houston had served Austin and Travis County well for over twenty years with mail and passenger service. Courtesy of Austin-Travis County Collection, Austin Public Library

Peck's Hall, located at Brazos and Pecan (Sixth) streets, occupied the site that later became the Driskill Hotel. Peck's was a popular meeting place, and for many years was headquarters of one of Austin's firefighting companies. Leather buckets and a hand-drawn fire truck were among the firefighting equipment stored at Peck's. Courtesy of Barker Texas History Center, University of Texas at Austin

Workmen labored many hours to make East Avenue one of Austin's main thoroughfares. This 1871 photo captures E. Canniff's road crew at work. Courtesy of Austin-Travis County Collection, Austin Public Library

This view looking up Congress Avenue was taken in the early 1870s. Courtesy of Austin-Travis County Collection, Austin Public Library

The Raymond House was one of Austin's finest hotels in the 1870s. It was built primarily to house the military officers who were stationed here after the Civil War. Located at Congress Avenue and Cedar (Fourth) Street, the Raymond House was best known for its saloon. Courtesy of Austin-Travis County Collection, Austin Public Library

The grandstand in Hyde Park was built in 1872. For many years the horse races at the Hyde Park track were one of Austin's most famous sporting attractions. Courtesy of Austin-Travis County Collection, Austin Public Library

A musical group of the 1870s. Left to right: Misters Culoman, Erwin, Quiner, Townsend, Holmes, and Oliphant. Courtesy of Austin-Travis County Collection, Austin Public Library

There was always excitement around the railway station in the 1870s. Mule-cars and carriages were present to serve the steady stream of arriving passengers. Courtesy of Austin-Travis County Collection, Austin Public Library

The most valuable commodity owned by many Austinites was a horse. Not only used for work or transportation, the horse was a favorite form of recreation also. These animals are receiving the finest care from Rankins Livery Stable at Trinity and Pecan (Sixth) streets. Courtesy of Austin-Travis County Collection, Austin Public Library

The International and Great Northern Railroad expanded in the 1870s and was Austin's major rail line for many years. This is a photo of the I.&G.N. Depot on Cypress (Third) Street. Courtesy of Austin-Travis County Collection, Austin Public Library

Sam Bass, pictured in the center, was one of America's most notorious outlaws. Bass lived in the Austin and Round Rock area when not robbing banks or trains. According to legend, Jesse and Frank James also practiced their trade in the Austin vicinity by robbing a train on its way to San Antonio. And in 1875 everyone in Austin knew that the dangerous John Wesley Harding was hiding out in the hills west of town. Courtesy of Austin-Travis County Collection, Austin Public Library

Cowboys take a break at Doan's Store, located on the Chisholm Trail. The Chisholm Trail, which ran along a line just twenty miles west of Austin, was the major route taken by South Texas cattlemen who drove their steers to the railhead in Kansas. Courtesy of Austin-Travis County Collection, Austin Public Library

The Texas German and English Academy was one of Austin's finest schools during the nineteenth century. It began in 1870 as the Texas Military Institute and was located at Colorado and Walnut (Fourteenth) streets. For many years it was headed by the well-respected and well-loved Professor Jacob Bickler. Courtesy of Austin-Travis County Collection, Austin Public Library

This is the home of Governor Edmund J. Davis, who served during the Reconstruction period from 1870 until 1874. Being both a Republican and a former Union cavalry officer, Davis was one of Texas' most unpopular governors. Courtesy of Austin-Travis County Collection, Austin Public Library

Austin's busiest intersection has always been Congress and Pecan (Sixth) Street. Giesen's Central Drug Store opened there in 1875 and was the place to purchase "chemicals and patent medicines." Courtesy of Austin-Travis County Collection, Austin Public Library

Nineteenth century architecture in Austin was dominated by elegance, grace, and craftsmanship. The residence of jeweler Carl Mayer was surely one of Austin's more unique designs. Courtesy of Austin-Travis County Collection, Austin Public Library

The Constitutional Convention of 1875 met in Austin and wrote the constitution that governs modern-day Texas. It was approved by the people of Texas in 1876. Courtesy of Austin-Travis County Collection, Austin Public Library

The view down Eleventh Street shows another view of the Courthouse. On the left is the building used for the County Jail. Courtesy of Austin-Travis County Collection, Austin Public Library

A family picnic can still be found on any spring or summer day in Austin. Part of the festivities for this group included a scenic tour of Austin on the J.D. Banton Moving and Excursion Car. Courtesy of Austin-Travis County Collection, Austin Public Library

The Travis County Courthouse from 1876 to 1930 was located at Eleventh Street and Congress. For many of those years, the Courthouse Saloon next door was probably a more pleasant meeting place for lawyers and their clients. Courtesy of Austin-Travis County Collection, Austin Public Library

...of Swedish settlers in the Austin vicinity. Most of these people are related to Swen Swenson and Swante Palm, two of Austin's first Swedish immigrants. Courtesy of Austin-Travis County Collection, Austin Public Library

Chapter 4
The Gilded Age: 1877~1900

Austin residents gathered at the head of Congress Avenue in 1881 to watch the Capitol burn. Courtesy of Austin-Travis County Collection, Austin Public Library

The Millet Opera House at 110 Ash (Ninth) Street was built in 1878 by Captain C.F. Millet, contractor and lumber yard owner. Plays, operas, banquets, and conventions were held at the Millet until the turn of the century. Edwin Booth and Lillie Langtry were two of the famous actors who performed there. Courtesy of Austin-Travis County Collection, Austin Public Library

This is a view of the old Capitol building after it had burned. A janitor started the fire when sparks began jumping from a pile of trash he was burning. Courtesy of Austin-Travis County Collection, Austin Public Library

The latter part of the nineteenth century in America was a time of industrial growth and technological advance. Evidence of this new age of gold and glitter could be witnessed throughout Austin. By 1880, the new technology had brought street lighting to the avenues, as well as sidewalks, cobblestone gutters, several new bridges, mule-driven streetcars, and every imaginable industry to serve Austin's growing needs. Hotels, bank buildings, and majestic new church structures filled the skyline. The state government was also expanding, which meant that businesses in town were flourishing from state contracts.

Then on November 9, 1881, the state government was dealt a serious blow. The Capitol building caught fire and within three hours was completely destroyed. Temporary offices were found for the state employees in various Austin houses and businesses, and the government attempted to continue operations as usual. The governor moved to the Travis County Courthouse, and the secretary of state established his new office in the county jail. Many Austinites viewed the tragic fire as a blessing in disguise. The editor of the satiric newspaper *Texas Siftings* expressed the opinion of many when he commented: "The architectural monstrosity that has so long disfigured the heaven-kissing hill at the head of Congress Avenue is no more."

Plans were underway for a new Capitol building even before the old one burned. Construction was completed in 1888, and the massive structure instantly became the pride of all Texans. The building was constructed of red granite blocks obtained from Granite Mountain near Marble Falls and shipped to Austin by rail. The height of the dome is 309 feet, 7 feet higher than the United States Capitol.

Another monumental event of the 1880s was the founding of the University of Texas. The establishment of a state university had been discussed since the days of the Republic, but the Civil War, lack of funds, and legislative opposition delayed the creation of the University until 1881. Even after funds were appropriated and construction had begun in Austin, there were still voices of opposition in the state legislature. One legislator expressed his displeasure when he proclaimed "holy horror at the idea of bringing up children on Congress Avenue in this city."

On September 15, 1883, the University of Texas officially began classes with 13 professors and over 200 students. Classes met at the temporary state capitol building until the following year, when the University's Main Building was completed. Additional classroom buildings were soon added, and within fifteen years the UT enrollment approached 1,000 students. The University has undoubtedly contributed more to the unique character of Austin than any institution or individual in its history.

Public school education was instituted in Texas as a result of the Constitution of 1876. Austin's first public school was located at Rio Grande and College Avenue (Twelfth Street). First known as the West Austin School, it became the Pease School in 1902. Students paid tuition, from $1.50 to $3.00 monthly, in order to subsidize the teachers' salaries. The Pease School is still operating at the same location and is the oldest school building in continuous use in Texas for public school purposes.

Two individuals in Austin at this time left a lasting impression on the history and the folklore of the city. Roaming the streets in the 1880s were two of Austin's most famous citizens, William Sidney Porter and Ben Thompson. William Sidney Porter came to Austin in the spring of 1884 and resided here for over fifteen years. He married a local girl, Athol Estes, and moved from job to job trying to support his young family. Porter sang in a local musical group and published his own satiric newspaper, *The Rolling Stone*. Criticized for many years as a worthless drifter, by the turn of the century Porter had gained worldwide recognition as America's premiere short story writer, O. Henry.

Ben Thompson, Austin city marshal in 1881 and 1882, was also a nationally known figure. Regarded in some circles as the best gunfighter in

Construction began on the Old Main Building at the University of Texas in 1882. Classes met at the temporary Capitol building until the Old Main was completed in 1884. Courtesy of Austin-Travis County Collection, Austin Public Library

Until the new Capitol building was constructed, state affairs were moved to this temporary Capitol, located at Congress Avenue and Eleventh. After 1888, it was used in various capacities by the public school system. Courtesy of Austin-Travis County Collection, Austin Public Library

the west, Thompson was known in Austin as the best gambler on Pecan Street. He became such a local hero that the Austin citizenry convinced him to try his hand at enforcing the law rather than breaking it. During his tenure as marshal, it was claimed that major crime dropped to an all-time low.

Above all else, Austin remained a political city. This was no more evident than in the 1880s and early 1890s. One of the major political movements in United States history began in the Central Texas region. The Southern Farmers Alliance, a rural political organization, was created in Lampasas in 1875. The Alliance spread through the South and the mid-West during the 1880s, and by 1886 it had grown into a national political force, the Populist Party. The Populists had emerged to challenge the industrial power brokers of the east and to reform the political system from an agrarian perspective. Members of the Travis County Farmers Alliance became leaders of the Texas Populist Party and in 1892 helped draft a national Populist platform. Their proposals for the protection and promotion of rural interests affected national politics for over twenty years.

At the same time that farmers yearned for a simpler, rural existence, Austin was fast becoming a complex urban center. The Austin telephone exchange opened in 1881. By 1887, the Edison Electric Light Company furnished indoor electric lighting to those who could afford it. The following year, electric streetlamps were installed in downtown Austin. Gas heating became available in 1889. And with the beginning of electric streetcar service in 1891, Austin could boast of the same modern conveniences as any city in the world. When thirty-one "artificial moonlight" towers were installed in 1894, many residents proudly proclaimed Austin more advanced than most cities in the world.

One of Austin's proudest moments came in 1893 with the completion of a new dam on the Colorado River just west of town. It was claimed to be the largest in the world and was believed to be the solution to the constant flooding of the river. The lake created by the dam was named Lake McDonald in honor of Austin's mayor. The area became a favorite recreation spot and tourist attraction. Several steamboats, the *Ben Hur*, the *Belle of Austin*, the *Chautauqua*, and the *Dixie*, cruised back and forth across the lake serving thousands of picnickers and sightseers.

As the new century began, tragedy struck Austin. In 1900, a devastating flood destroyed the dam, the lake, the steamboats, and hundreds of homes. But the optimism of earlier days prevailed, and Austin began to rebuild.

Ben Thompson was one of Austin's most famous, and certainly most colorful, nineteenth-century citizens. He was city marshall in the early 1880s, but he had to resign in order to face murder charges in San Antonio. By his own admission, Thompson claimed to have killed thirty-two men. Bat Masterson once remarked that there was "no man living who equalled Ben Thompson with a pistol." Thompson died where he had always been most comfortable, in a saloon shootout. Courtesy of Austin-Travis County Collection, Austin Public Library

The first residence hall built on the UT campus was called B Hall. Completed in 1890, B Hall was constructed with funds donated by George Brackenridge. Rooms rented for $6 a month, and board ran from $8 to $12. Card playing and drinking of liquor were expressly forbidden. Courtesy of Austin-Travis County Collection, Austin Public Library

The University begins recruiting fans at an early age. Courtesy of Austin-Travis County Collection, Austin Public Library

The present Brackenridge Hospital came into being in 1883. It was called the City and County Hospital, and it was located at the corner of Sabine and Walnut (Fourteenth) streets. A check of hospital records in the 1880s indicates most hospital patients suffered from smallpox, scarlet fever, or diphtheria. Courtesy of Austin-Travis County Collection, Austin Public Library

George W. Littlefield served with Terry's Texas Rangers during the Civil War and returned to Texas a war hero. He became a successful cattleman, banker, and hotel owner. Major Littlefield is best remembered for his love of and contributions to the University of Texas. He served as regent at UT, and he donated both land and money to the University. Courtesy of Austin-Travis County Collection, Austin Public Library

Nurses congregate in front of the St. David's Hospital, which was located at the corner of Rio Grande and Seventeenth streets. Courtesy of Austin-Travis County Collection, Austin Public Library

UT co-eds at one time took their breaks between classes by having tea in the bluebonnet fields. Courtesy of Austin-Travis County Collection, Austin Public Library

University of Texas faculty, 1884. Courtesy of Austin-Travis County Collection, Austin Public Library

Traffic on the Congress Avenue Bridge was usually light in the 1880s. These Austin folks are enjoying a leisurely stroll across the bridge and are approaching First Street. It was not always so tranquil or safe. In 1883, a herd of cattle met a mule-drawn wagon on the bridge and a stampede occurred. Part of the bridge gave way, hundreds of cattle drowned, and the bridge was out of commission for several months. Courtesy of Austin-Travis County Collection, Austin Public Library

No institution is more vital to a community than a free and courageous newspaper. The Austin American Statesman, known for a long period as the Democratic Statesman, has served Austin for nearly a century. Note that the early Statesman building was in the same building as a beer distributor. The church on the left was the First Baptist. Courtesy of Austin-Travis County Collection, Austin Public Library

This photo looking north on Congress was probably taken around 1885. In the background, construction on the Capitol appears about half finished. Courtesy of Austin-Travis County Collection, Austin Public Library

Construction on the present State Capitol Building began in 1882. This 1884 photo shows the construction in process. Note the Old Main Building at the University in the background. Courtesy of Austin-Travis County Collection, Austin Public Library

The city has not always been in the trash collection business. This old man in the 1880s made his living by hauling trash and junk for Austin residents and businesses. Courtesy of Austin-Travis County Collection, Austin Public Library

V.O. Weed ran two of Austin's most flourishing businesses from his building on East Eighth Street. He operated a stable on the ground floor, and upstairs he conducted an undertaking business. Courtesy of Austin-Travis County Collection, Austin Public Library

The Breggerhoff Building, which housed the Capital Business College on its third floor, is pictured in this 1885 photo. The view is a southern look down Congress. Courtesy of Austin-Travis County Collection, Austin Public Library

The toll bridge over the Colorado cost $80,000 to construct. The cost to walk over the bridge was 5¢, and for another nickel you could take your horse. In June of 1886, the city bought the bridge and eliminated the toll charge. To celebrate, Austinites held a parade and barbecue. Courtesy of Austin-Travis County Collection, Austin Public Library

Austin High School graduates of 1887. Courtesy of Austin-Travis County Collection, Austin Public Library

The Hill City Quartette never achieved fortune and fame as a singing group in the 1880s. One of their members, Will Porter (left front), would find fame and fortune as writer O.Henry. C.E. Hillyer sits beside Porter; behind them are, left to right, R.H. Edmondson and H.H. Long. Courtesy of Austin-Travis County Collection, Austin Public Library

The Driskill Hotel, built in 1886 by cattle baron Jesse L. Driskill, has been called the finest hotel in the south. The Austin paper once claimed that the Driskill should be exempt from paying taxes because it had done so much for Austin's reputation. Courtesy of Austin-Travis County Collection, Austin Public Library

The new Capitol building was completed and dedicated in 1888. Before the Goddess of Liberty was raised to the top of the Capitol dome, workers from the construction crews gathered around the statue for this picture. Courtesy of Austin-Travis County Collection, Austin Public Library

The Governor's Mansion at Eleventh Street and Colorado is viewed in this 1888 photo taken from the new Capitol. The governor residing there at this time was L.S. (Sul) Ross, a famous Texas Ranger and Civil War veteran. He was also widely known for rescuing from the Comanches Cynthia Ann Parker, mother of the famous Indian leader Quanah Parker. Courtesy of Austin-Travis County Collection, Austin Public Library

The Austin Board of Trade was created in 1887, and it was later headquartered in this building at the northeast corner of Congress and Cedar (Fourth) streets. The board was the forerunner of the Chamber of Commerce. Courtesy of Austin-Travis County Collection, Austin Public Library

Music festivals and public songfests have long been a part of Austin's tradition. This arch over Congress Avenue was erected in 1889 to welcome German singing societies from all parts of Texas to a "saengerfest." Austin's Saengerrunde, a German folk-singing group, and the Austin Musical Union had been created ten years earlier. Courtesy of Austin-Travis County Collection, Austin Public Library

New rail lines for the streetcars are being installed on Congress Avenue. Courtesy of Austin-Travis County Collection, Austin Public Library

The main building at St. Edward's University was originally built in 1889. Even though it was destroyed twice, once by fire and once by tornado, it still retains the basic design perceived by its founders. St. Edward's began in 1872 as St. Edward's Academy. Father Sorin of Notre Dame and Mary Doyle donated land to the school, and by 1885 it was a chartered school occupying a beautiful campus in South Austin. Courtesy of Austin-Travis County Collection, Austin Public Library

The Austin Street Railway Company began electric streetcar operations in 1891. The company, started by Hyde Park developer Monroe M. Shipe, continued to transport Austin citizens by streetcar until 1940. This photograph portrays the throng of onlookers who came out to witness the first day of operations for the streetcars. Courtesy of Austin-Travis County Collection, Austin Public Library

Mule-driven streetcars were Austin's main form of public transportation for years. They slowly disappeared from city streets after electric streetcars made their appearance in 1891. In this photo both forms of mass transit seem to be co-existing quite well. Courtesy of Austin-Travis County Collection, Austin Public Library

Elisabet Ney Museum. Courtesy of Robyn Turner

Elisabet Ney, European born and trained, was a world-renowned sculptor in the nineteenth century. She and her husband moved to Texas in the 1870s. In 1892, Ney permanently settled in Austin and built her internationally known studio, Formosa. This studio is now the Elisabet Ney Museum and is located at Forty-Fourth and Avenue G in Austin. The statues of Stephen F. Austin and Sam Houston in the State Capitol Building were exhibited by Elisabet Ney in the 1893 World's Fair. Courtesy of Austin-Travis County Collection, Austin Public Library

Local women pose at the dedication ceremonies of a monument to Terry's Texas Rangers, an Austin-based Confederate fighting unit. Courtesy of Austin-Travis County Collection, Austin Public Library

The Palm School was constructed in 1892 and was called the Tenth Ward School for several years. Its location at First Street and East Avenue had been the old arsenal site dating back to the days of the Republic. The army gave the site to the city of Austin with the stipulation it be used only for the public school system. Courtesy of Austin-Travis County Collection, Austin Public Library

Football came to the University in 1893. This first team of Longhorns was barely more than an intramural team, but their expressions indicate that they took the game as seriously as modern-day players. Courtesy of Austin-Travis County Collection, Austin Public Library

Hyde Park was flat and open countryside until developers moved in near the end of the century. Courtesy of Austin-Travis County Collection, Austin Public Library

The Hyde Park Pavilion was a favorite recreation spot in Austin. The lake at the pavilion was the site of swimming, sailing, rowing, and an occasional revival. Courtesy of Austin-Travis County Collection, Austin Public Library

Hyde Park was developed by Monroe Shipe, the man riding in this horse-drawn carriage. A lot in Hyde Park could be purchased for $125 in the 1890s. Courtesy of Austin-Travis County Collection, Austin Public Library

In addition to being a racetrack site, Hyde Park was the scene of sham battles (war games). Spectators would fill the grandstand to watch the action as seen in this 1894 photo. Courtesy of Austin-Travis County Collection, Austin Public Library

Students of the Hornsby Bend School appear in this photograph from the 1890s. The teacher at the upper right is Martha Miner Faulk. Courtesy of Anne C. McAfee

Even though Hyde Park was several miles from downtown, streetcars ran there because of the racetrack and the military encampment. The fact that the developer of Hyde Park also owned the transit system might explain the good service. Courtesy of Austin-Travis County Collection, Austin Public Library

In May of 1895, Austin's "artificial moonlight" towers were first turned on. Thirty-one towers were originally set up throughout Austin to light the hilly streets. They were purchased from the city of Detroit in exchange for the railroad tracks used to transport materials to the dam west of town. Nearly all of the towers are still in operation today. Author photo

Legislators leave the Capitol and walk south to Congress Avenue during a rare Austin snowfall in 1895. Courtesy of Austin-Travis County Collection, Austin Public Library

These young ladies were students at Tillotson College in 1896. This photo was taken in front of Allen Hall on the campus. Courtesy of Austin-Travis County Collection, Austin Public Library

One year after losing the presidential election, William Jennings Bryan visited Austin and was taken on a panther hunt by former Governor James Hogg. Both Governor Hogg (in the middle on the white horse) and Bryan (on Hogg's left) portrayed themselves as champions of the common man. Courtesy of Austin-Travis County Collection, Austin Public Library

On July 7, 1896, thousands of people assembled on the Capitol grounds to watch the dedication of the Firemen's Monument. For many years every celebration or dedication would begin with a parade down Congress Avenue and culminate with a speech on the Capitol grounds. Courtesy of Austin-Travis County Collection, Austin Public Library

The Hancock Opera House, the building pictured at center, opened in 1896 and was called the hub of cultural entertainment in Texas. Owned by Mayor Lewis Hancock, it was located at 120 West Sixth Street. Among the famous performers playing at the Hancock were John Barrymore, John Philip Sousa, Lillian Russell, and Anna Pavlova. To the left of the opera house is the U.S. Post Office Building, and to its right is the Austin National Bank. Courtesy of Austin-Travis County Collection, Austin Public Library

The teller in the bank cage is William Sydney Porter, better known as O.Henry. O.Henry held many jobs in Austin before his fame as a writer took him to New York. His banking career ended rather unpleasantly when he was sent to prison in 1896 for embezzlement. O.Henry continually pleaded his innocence, but after he left prison a world-famous author, it seemed to matter very little. Courtesy of Austin-Travis County Collection, Austin Public Library

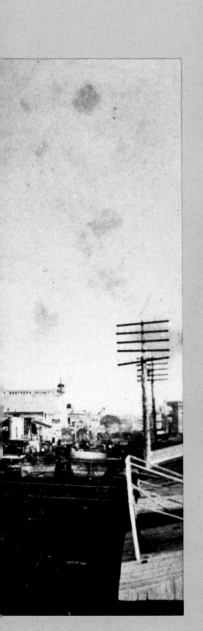

5.8.98.

Many of the soldiers at this Hyde Park encampment in 1898 would soon see action in the Spanish-American War. Their minds were surely on the lady visitors to their camp and not on the war during this spring afternoon. Courtesy of Austin-Travis County Collection, Austin Public Library

When Raatz Department Store held a "mid-summer clearance sale," it appeared as if everyone in Austin came to find a bargain. This 1898 photo was taken in the 400 block of Congress Avenue. Courtesy of Austin-Travis County Collection, Austin Public Library

High school classes were held in this building from 1899 until 1916. The Allan High School was located at the corner of Trinity and Ninth Street. It became a junior high in 1916 when the Stephen F. Austin High School opened at Twelfth and Rio Grande. Courtesy of Austin-Travis County Collection, Austin Public Library

Congress Avenue and Pecan (Sixth) Street, 1898. Courtesy of Austin-Travis County Collection, Austin Public Library

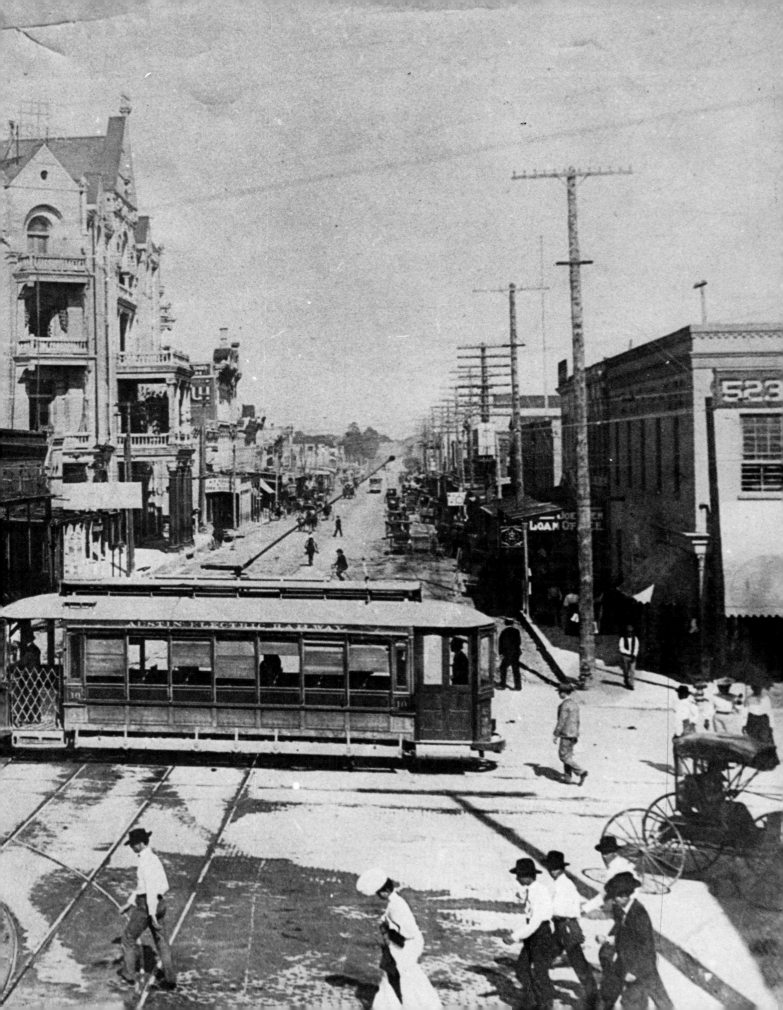

In 1899 the building that served as temporary Capitol from 1881 until 1888 burned. At the time of the fire it was being used by the school system for needed classroom space. Courtesy of Barker Texas History Center, University of Texas at Austin

C-18

At the turn of the century one of America's most notable citizens, Booker T. Washington, visited Austin. Washington was a guest of the Ebenezer Baptist Church, and he is shown here at a banquet at the St. John's Orphan Home. Washington is seated on the right in the company of several of the Black community's religious leaders. Courtesy of Austin-Travis County Collection, Austin Public Library

The Ben Hur was one of Austin's most exciting attractions. The steamboat is shown here at the edge of the dam before the flood of 1900. The lake created by the dam was called Lake McDonald. Courtesy of Austin-Travis County Collection, Austin Public Library

For fifty cents you could take the three-and-a-half hour cruise of the Colorado River on the Ben Hur. In the evenings dances were held on its decks. Courtesy of Austin-Travis County Collection, Austin Public Library

The land to the east of East Avenue was undeveloped for many years. This 1900 photo depicts a bogged-down wagon on Chicon Street. Courtesy of Austin-Travis County Collection, Austin Public Library

Strolling across the dam was not an everyday occurrence. This man made headlines with this daredevil, if not foolhardy, feat in the 1890s. Note the Ben Hur in the background on Lake McDonald. Courtesy of Austin-Travis County Collection, Austin Public Library

Lake McDonald. The railroad ran alongside the shoreline to deliver supplies to the various construction projects on the lake. Courtesy of Austin-Travis County Collection, Austin Public Library

96

Debris from the flood was scattered all along the shore of Lake McDonald. Houses, boats, docks, and even automobiles were tossed against rock banks and completely destroyed by the floodwaters. Courtesy of Austin-Travis County Collection, Austin Public Library

After the flood of 1900, Austin residents flocked to the broken dam to survey the damage. This group made the event a family outing. Courtesy of Austin-Travis County Collection, Austin Public Library

The floodwaters completely engulfed the Deep Eddy recreation area and bath house. Courtesy of Austin-Travis County Collection, Austin Public Library

No invention has had greater impact on American life than that of the automobile. One of the first in Austin was owned by the Reinhold Haschke family, shown here at the Capitol in 1903. Courtesy of Austin-Travis County Collection, Austin Public Library

Chapter 5
A New Century: 1900 ~ 1929

Austinites jammed Congress Avenue to watch the parade to honor President McKinley. Governor Joseph Sayers is riding in the carriage with the President. Courtesy of Austin-Travis County Collection, Austin Public Library

Texas Independence Day has traditionally been celebrated at the University by firing cannon salutes. These students gathered at the Old Main Building on March 2, 1903. Courtesy of Austin-Travis County Collection, Austin Public Library

The first decade of the twentieth century brought new opportunities and new challenges to the city of Austin. In addition to the destruction left by the flood of 1900, expansion of the University and the state government presented an array of problems. As the University outgrew its original forty acres, funding priorities escalated into political controversies. As the tide of progressive reform swept the nation, the whole concept of the role of the state bureaucracy began to be questioned. The result in both cases was growth and expansion, and the city of Austin bore the consequences, the bad as well as the good.

Growth and progress became synonymous in the first years of the new century. The electric streetcar system expanded its operation as far north as the Hyde Park section, Austin's first suburb. A new concrete bridge was built over the river at Congress Avenue. By 1910, Austin had its own skyscrapers, the Scarbrough and Littlefield buildings. The horseless carriage was no longer considered an intrusion into the lives of "civilized" people, and as early as 1910 the automobile was an invaluable part of Austin's lifestyle and economy. When the first airplane landed in Austin in 1911, the twentieth century had really arrived.

The widespread use of the automobile significantly changed the character of social life in Austin. Sunday afternoon picnics now included drives to the river, Pease Park, Barton Springs, or Onion Creek. Critics of the automobile claimed it was destroying the family and corrupting the youth. The other corrupting factor in society was alcohol, and by 1910 the national progressive movement turned its attention to eliminating its influence.

As the center of political debate in Texas, Austin had heard the arguments for and against prohibition many times. As long as local option was the law, there was no doubt Austin would remain wet. Austin had always been accused of having more taverns per capita than any city in the state. The thriving saloons on Sixth Street were proof that the charge was true. The red light district on West Second Street was also prosperous, to the dismay of the reformers. In fact, it was so prosperous and so conspicuous that the city fathers shut it down in 1915. By 1918, the prohibitionists had allied themselves politically with the women's movement, and prohibition became law in Texas. The next year it became law in the United States with the passage of the Eighteenth Amendment.

The other major political debate of the period was the issue of women's suffrage. Austin women were at the forefront of the battle to gain both public and legislative support. Four of the more notable women in that group included Mrs. A. Caswell Ellis, Mrs. Frederick Eby, Mrs. Dave Doom, and Mrs. Arthur McCallum. Jane Yelvington McCallum came to symbolize the Austin contingent of strong and intelligent women who refused to accept anything less than their full political rights. With the passage of the Nineteenth Amendment, Texas' archaic election laws were abandoned. No longer did the Texas Election Code prohibit the voting of "paupers, aliens, idiots, imbeciles, criminals, and women."

By the end of 1915, political rhetoric in Austin's government halls, restaurants, and taverns turned to international events. Local and state issues seemed insignificant when compared to events in Europe. Soon World War I became a reality, and in 1918 Austinites began to share in the suffering of millions of Europeans.

Since 1890, Camp Mabry in West Austin has been an encampment for the forces of the Texas National Guard. During World War I, it was utilized as a training center for army recruits. The University, which had various military contracts and obligations, also used Camp Mabry as a supply and storage center. Parades to and from Camp Mabry became commonplace during the war years. It made no difference whether "the boys" were leaving for the war or returning from it. When the Armistice came on November 11, 1918, Austinites packed Congress Avenue to celebrate. Throughout the merriment, however, there was always the haunting silence of those who did not return.

The census of 1920 calculated the Austin population at 34,000. This number would swell to over 53,000 during the decade of the Roaring Twenties. However, not everyone was "roaring," especially the small farmers and rural laborers. Low farm prices and high rural unemployment sent thousands of Texans to the cities. Austin, with its stable work force and its apparent prosperity, received many of these emigrants from the farmlands. The source of this prosperity was, of course, the state government and the University.

Despite the general conservatism of the average Texan, more demands were placed on the state government for public services, especially in the areas of highway construction and public education. As the state provided more and more of these services, Austin's economy benefitted. In 1928 a ten-year plan for physical improvements in the city was drawn up. City services expanded at this time with the creation of a planned park system and a city recreation department. The city government was thriving, business was booming, and the University was striking it rich.

Oil was discovered on University-owned lands in West Texas in the late 1920s. This bonanza poured millions of dollars into the school's general fund. The University was generating more revenue than it literally knew what to do with. Elaborate construction projects were begun in hopes of creating "the greatest university in the South." Seven new dormitories were built, a gymnasium constructed, and a new library planned.

Private business was also flourishing. The *Austin American* daily reminded its readers of the building boom by running a tally of new housing and business structures. Every Sunday the newspaper printed a special supplement entitled "Austin Progress" or "Today's Skyline." The emphasis was on growth, building, and progress — with each seemingly defined as the same. Even the farmers were claiming prosperity. Bumper crops and a natural rise in prices made 1928 the most profitable farming year of the decade.

Austin, and indeed the entire country, had no premonition of future events. All anyone could see were rises in population, bank receipts, building permits, government contracts, and the spirits of the people. Within the coming year, however, the prospect of future prosperity would become economic chaos.

The Model A and the horse-and-buggy existed together for only a few years after the turn of the century. Courtesy of Austin-Travis County Collection, Austin Public Library

Four generations of Austinites, left to right: Henry Emil Seekatz, Wilhelm Seekatz, Henry Seekatz, and William Seekatz. Courtesy of Henry Seekatz

President Theodore Roosevelt, in his carriage, appears to be surrounded by several cautious Secret Service men during his 1905 visit to Austin. Courtesy of Austin-Travis County Collection, Austin Public Library

The Seekatz Meat Market was located at the southeast corner of Fourteenth Street and Lavaca. Courtesy of Henry Seekatz

The flag flies high over Congress Avenue in 1905. Courtesy of Austin-Travis County Collection, Austin Public Library

Congress Avenue was paved with bricks in 1905. While workers are busily completing the job, city council members gather to receive the plaudits. Courtesy of Austin-Travis County Collection, Austin Public Library

This 1906 photo shows two of Austin's impressive church structures. On the left is the Tenth Street Methodist Church, and on the right is St. Mary's Cathedral. Courtesy of Austin-Travis County Collection, Austin Public Library

Philip Bosche operated Bosche's Troy Laundry at 705 Congress Avenue. Courtesy of Austin-Travis County Collection, Austin Public Library

St. John's Orphanage was home for several generations of young girls and boys. The orphanage was located "way out north of town," a spot now the home of Highland Mall. Courtesy of Austin-Travis County Collection, Austin Public Library

Austinites of an earlier generation wore formal attire when attending a party. Courtesy of Austin-Travis County Collection, Austin Public Library

Ceiling fans, brass rails, and Barton Springs Whiskies were featured at this saloon. *Courtesy of Austin-Travis County Collection, Austin Public Library*

Whenever the streetcar system opened a new route, city fathers and railway owners would mark the occasion with a speech and the first ride. This meeting celebrated the first railway routes to South Austin. *Courtesy of Austin-Travis County Collection, Austin Public Library*

This musical entourage is pictured at the Two Brothers Saloon at San Marcos and Sixth streets. Austin residents of every ethnic background mixed freely in this area, one of two major red-light districts in town. The other location where "bawdyhouses" flourished was on West Second Street, just two blocks off Congress. Courtesy of Felicia Buratti Pecora

This is a view of East Avenue before it was paved. It is now Interstate 35. Courtesy of Austin-Travis County Collection, Austin Public Library

Scarbrough's Department Store has been a landmark in Austin since E.M. Scarbrough came to town in 1889. The Scarbrough Building at Sixth Street and Congress was Austin's first skyscraper after its construction in 1910. Courtesy of Austin-Travis County Collection, Austin Public Library

Flags and decorations draped Harrell and Klein's Clothing Store on Christmas Day of 1910. Courtesy of Austin-Travis County Collection, Austin Public Library

Austin honored its firefighting forces in this 1910 parade. Volunteers served in Austin's fire companies until 1916, when full-time, salaried firemen took over. Courtesy of Austin-Travis County Collection, Austin Public Library

A concrete bridge was
constructed over the
Colorado River at Congress
Avenue in 1910. Courtesy of
Austin-Travis County Collec-
tion, Austin Public Library

Local marksmen, with their
guns and trophies in hand.
Courtesy of Henry Seekatz

A picnic in 1911 was the
occasion for this picture of
UT faculty children. Courtesy
of Barker Texas History
Center, University of Texas at
Austin.

Picnics near Barton Springs have been an Austin tradition since its inception. Courtesy of Austin-Travis County Collection, Austin Public Library

The Caswell family reunion, 1911. Courtesy of Austin-Travis County Collection, Austin Public Library

Two Austin ladies appear to be enjoying a leisurely drive. Courtesy of Austin-Travis County Collection, Austin Public Library

Crowds gathered in 1911 to witness the first plane to land in Austin, brought here under the sponsorship of Will Caswell. Courtesy of Austin-Travis County Collection, Austin Public Library

Picture made 1911
Reading left to right

Horseshoeing businesses used to be as common as gas stations are today. They did a thriving business well into the twentieth century. Pictured in 1911 are, left to right: Charley Bulian, James Hart, Mr. Barber, Kerry Smith, and Mrs. Barber (in wagon). Courtesy of Austin-Travis County Collection, Austin Public Library

Austin City Commission in 1912. Courtesy of Austin-Travis County Collection, Austin Public Library

In 1913, streetcars were
serving all of downtown
Austin with efficient and
non-polluting transportation.
Courtesy of Austin-Travis
County Collection, Austin
Public Library

Nothing could excite Austin
children more than a pony
ride through Pease Park.
Courtesy of Austin-Travis
County Collection, Austin
Public Library

Football was first played at the University in 1893. It did not become an official UT sport until 1898, when the first coach, D.J. Edwards, was hired. In this 1913 game against Notre Dame, UT's Paul Simmons dives for extra yardage. Courtesy of Austin-Travis County Collection, Austin Public Library

This Texas hill country cowboy would not only grow up to be one of Austin's most prominent citizens, but he would also be president of the United States. Courtesy of Austin-Travis County Collection, Austin Public Library

One of the older UT buildings still in use today is Garrison Hall, named for George Garrison, an early UT history professor. Courtesy of Austin-Travis County Collection, Austin Public Library

The University of Texas Law School has grown in size and stature in the twentieth century. This photo depicts the first UT Law School Building on campus. Today the UT Law School is exceeded in enrollment and expenditure by only one other institution in the country, Harvard. Courtesy of Barker Texas History Center, University of Texas at Austin

The Old Main Building looking north along University Avenue. Courtesy of Barker Texas History Center, University of Texas at Austin

Parking at the University was not always a problem. These students had no trouble finding a space in the center of campus. Courtesy of Austin-Travis County Collection, Austin Public Library

The 1915 flood left Sixth Street impassable from the swollen banks of Shoal Creek. Courtesy of Austin-Travis County Collection, Austin Public Library

Floodwaters destroyed hundreds of homes and made travel impossible on city streets. Courtesy of Austin-Travis County Collection, Austin Public Library

The Shriners held their first parade in Austin in 1913 to welcome the circus to town. Proceeds from the event went to help support programs for needy children in the Travis County area. Courtesy of Austin-Travis County Collection, Austin Public Library

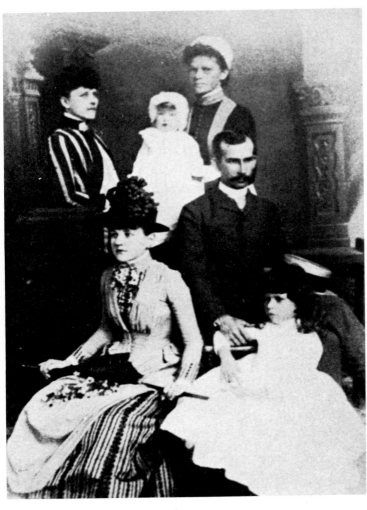

Clara Driscoll Sevier built this home in 1916 on the shores of Lake Austin and deeded it to the Texas Fine Arts Commission in 1943. Renovated in the early sixties and renamed the Laguna Gloria Art Museum, today it is one of Austin's most cherished cultural landmarks. Courtesy of Austin-Travis County Collection, Austin Public Library

President Woodrow Wilson's most trusted adviser and closest friend was Austinite Colonel Edward M. House, who had been the force behind the political fortunes of Governor Hogg in the 1890s. A classic example of the "backroom politician," he has been credited with creating the conservative Texas Democratic establishment. After leaving Texas politics in 1906, House moved to the national political arena and for several years was the second most influential and powerful man in the country.

This photo of Colonel House and his family was taken at their residence in Austin. Courtesy of Austin-Travis County Collection, Austin Public Library

Workmen clear debris out of Waller Creek following the devastating 1915 flood. Courtesy of Austin-Travis County Collection, Austin Public Library

William Jennings Bryan moved his family to Austin for two reasons. He had political allies here within the Democratic Party. The other reason concerned the health of his son. Doctors advised Bryan that the weather in the southwest would greatly aid his son's medical problems. Two of Bryan's boys are pictured here with their chauffeurs at the Capital City Garage. Courtesy of Austin-Travis County Collection, Austin Public Library

Another Austin citizen, Albert Sidney Burleson, was also a close political ally of President Wilson. Burleson served in Wilson's cabinet as postmaster general. Burleson is visiting in this photo with William Jennings Bryan (right), the acknowledged leader of the Democratic Party from 1896 to 1912. Bryan also lived in Austin for nearly a year. Courtesy of Austin-Travis County Collection, Austin Public Library

After successful ventures into the hill country, hunters made a tradition of displaying their kill at Petmecky's Sporting Goods. This hunting season occurred in 1916. Courtesy of Austin-Travis County Collection, Austin Public Library

Barton Springs has been labeled "the world's most beautiful swimming hole." It was named for William Barton, who moved to the area in 1837. This picture of Barton Springs before it was deeded to the city for a park shows the old mill of G.T. Rabb. Another Austin businessman, Michael Paggi, also had a grist mill, a bath house, and an ice plant at Barton Springs during the nineteenth century.

The beauty of the area along Barton Creek was recognized as early as 1730 when Franciscan priests built a mission at the location. It was only temporary, however, because of the constant threat of Indians. The Spanish mission system did flourish seventy miles down the road at San Antonio. Courtesy of Austin-Travis County Collection, Austin Public Library

The ice factory at Barton Springs provided residents south of the river with huge chunks of block ice, a luxury in nineteenth-century Austin. Courtesy of Austin-Travis County Collection, Austin Public Library

Governor Jim Ferguson and his wife, Miriam, were two of the most colorful, as well as controversial, politicians in Texas history. At the time of this photo in 1917, Pa and Ma Ferguson were being welcomed at the Austin railroad depot. Within a few months Governor Ferguson would be impeached for his questionable financial dealings. Courtesy of Austin-Travis County Collection, Austin Public Library

A.J. Zilker purchased the land around Barton Springs in the early 1900s and in 1917 gave the property to the city to be used as a park. This photo depicts the construction work necessary to transform Barton Springs and Zilker Park into the scenic public recreation areas they are today. Courtesy of Austin-Travis County Collection, Austin Public Library

Travis Heights has always been one of Austin's most beautiful neighborhoods. This 1917 entrance to Travis Heights was located at Riverside Drive and Alameda. Courtesy of Austin-Travis County Collection, Austin Public Library

During the war years, soldiers marching through the University campus were a common sight. Courtesy of Austin-Travis County Collection, Austin Public Library

During World War I, troops and supplies were transported in and out of Camp Mabry at a rapid rate. This train wreck slowed operations at the Army installation. Courtesy of Austin-Travis County Collection, Austin Public Library

Everyone was expected to do his or her part for the war effort. This storefront display in downtown Austin asked people to come in and sign a "wheatless pledge." The Allies in Europe needed as much wheat as possible, and thus Americans were encouraged to eat potatoes instead of wheat. Those who signed the pledge to go wheatless were called "Potato Patriots." Courtesy of Austin-Travis County Collection, Austin Public Library

Parades were held throughout the war years in Austin. In this photo, troops stationed at Camp Mabry were being honored. Courtesy of Austin-Travis County Collection, Austin Public Library

In this photo, Austin resident Fred Terrell proudly displays his army uniform before he returns to his unit. Courtesy of Clarksville Neighborhood Center

The Armistice to end World War I was signed on November 11, 1918. Austinites celebrated the victory with this parade on Congress Avenue. Courtesy of Austin-Travis County Collection, Austin Public Library

Although the automobile boom hit Austin before World War I, the horse and wagon remained on the scene for many years, as in this 1920 photo at Second Street and Congress Avenue. Courtesy of Austin-Travis County Collection, Austin Public Library

Automobiles were no longer oddities on the brick-paved streets of Austin in 1918. Courtesy of Austin-Travis County Collection, Austin Public Library

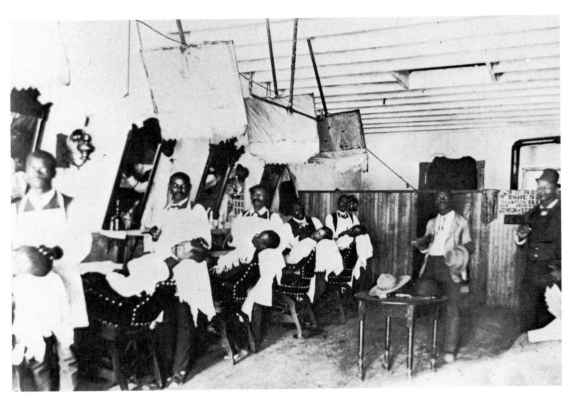

In the 1920s, a man could get a haircut for 35¢, a shave for 15¢, and a shampoo for 25¢. These customers also got fanned while in the barber chair. Courtesy of Austin-Travis County Collection, Austin Public Library

The opening of the Queen Theater in February of 1921 brought hundreds of Austinites to its premiere showing. Traffic on Congress was impassable as the crowds gathered. Courtesy of Austin-Travis County Collection, Austin Public Library

The Confederate Veterans Home was located on the 1500 block of West Sixth Street. Built in 1886, the home was constructed by and for veterans who served under General Hood in the Civil War. Courtesy of Austin-Travis County Collection, Austin Public Library

Women survivors of Confederate veterans also had a home in Austin. Both the men's and women's facilities were among the largest and finest of all such homes in the South. Courtesy of Austin-Travis County Collection, Austin Public Library

The Austin Street Railway Company served public transportation needs for fifty years. Courtesy of Austin-Travis County Collection, Austin Public Library

Governor Pat Neff was the Stephen F. Austin Hotel's first guest when it opened in 1924. Courtesy of Austin-Travis County Collection, Austin Public Library

Residents of the Texas Confederate Veterans Home pose for this 1921 photograph. Courtesy of Austin-Travis County Collection, Austin Public Library

Rainy Austin streets often mean an increase in accidents. In the 1920s, crowds gathered to watch this streetcar derailment. Courtesy of Austin-Travis County Collection, Austin Public Library

In the spring of 1922, two tornadoes struck Austin. One of the funnels can be seen hovering over the Capitol in this photo. Thirteen people were killed on that tragic day. Courtesy of Austin-Travis County Collection, Austin Public Library

Wrecking Crew
Lou Gehrig
Babe Ruth

Miriam A. Ferguson, known to everyone as "Ma," became Texas' first and only woman governor in 1925. She served one term and was then re-elected in 1933. Her husband, James Ferguson, had previously been governor but was impeached in 1917. This 1925 photo on the steps of the Governor's Mansion shows Ma Ferguson welcoming Will Rogers to Austin. Courtesy of Austin-Travis County Collection, Austin Public Library

Two genuine American heroes visited Austin in 1925. Babe Ruth (right) and Lou Gehrig accompanied their Yankee teammates and played an exhibition at Clark Field. Nationally known for its "centerfield cliff," Clark Field was the baseball home of the Longhorns until Disch-Falk Field was completed in 1974. Courtesy of Austin-Travis County Collection, Austin Public Library

In 1925 the Austin Country Club was located at Forty-First and Red River. That location is now the Hancock Golf Course. Courtesy of Austin-Travis County Collection, Austin Public Library

The All American Dance Orchestra provided music for Austin participants of the Jazz Age. Courtesy of Austin-Travis County Collection, Austin Public Library

Eight of Austin's "men in blue" pose for some well-deserved recognition in this 1926 photo at police headquarters. Courtesy of Austin-Travis County Collection, Austin Public Library

This Ku Klux Klan march in the 1920s appears to have attracted a substantial crowd in downtown Austin. However, Klan activity in Austin never achieved the acceptance that it did in other Texas cities. Courtesy of Austin-Travis County Collection, Austin Public Library

These covered wagons on the Capitol grounds are not transporting settlers west; they are part of a caravan of Texas farmers who came to Austin to protest low farm prices. Courtesy of Austin-Travis County Collection, Austin Public Library

The Pan American Center has played an important role in the social and recreational life of Austin's Mexican-American citizens. The Pan Am Center and adjacent park are part of the Austin Parks and Recreation Department, which was created in 1927. Courtesy of Austin-Travis County Collection, Austin Public Library

Prosperity in the 1920s was a reality for most Austin citizens. The center of that prosperity was, of course, Congress Avenue, the commercial and financial backbone of Austin. Courtesy of Austin-Travis County Collection, Austin Public Library

A costume party during the Roaring (?) Twenties. Courtesy of Austin-Travis County Collection, Austin Public Library

The home of John Swisher, early Austin businessman, was constructed in the 1850s in the 400 block of San Antonio. In 1928, it was moved and rebuilt by Dr. and Mrs Zachary T. Scott. The Scott residence, named Sweetbrush, is located at 2408 Sweetbrush. Courtesy of Austin-Travis County Collection, Austin Public Library

The hills west of Austin have supported hundreds of families while insulating them from the "advances" of city life. During the prohibition years, many of these families made their living from the sale of bootleg whiskey. Hundreds of stills were in operation west of town, perhaps family operations as in the case of this Bull Creek clan. Courtesy of Austin-Travis County Collection, Austin Public Library

The University Co-op has long been a landmark near the University campus. This 1927 photo depicts the streetcar service available to students at the time. Courtesy of Austin-Travis County Collection, Austin Public Library

These Huston College basketball players led their school to the state championship in 1928. Courtesy of Austin-Travis County Collection, Austin Public Library

This is a 1928 photo of the main building at Samuel Huston College. The Black institution of higher learning was founded in 1900 and merged with Tillotson College in 1952. Courtesy of Austin-Travis County Collection, Austin Public Library

No doubt proud of their accomplishments, the 1928 graduates of Sam Huston College pose on the steps of the college administration building. Courtesy of Austin-Travis County Collection, Austin Public Library

A new fleet of cars for sale was displayed on the "drag" in 1929. Note the billboards advising University students to "Graduate to Camels" and for "Your Health" a five-cent Dr. Pepper. Courtesy of Austin-Travis County Collection, Austin Public Library

The Neill-Cochran home at 2310 San Gabriel, shown during a 1929 snowfall, is the last of the surviving Greek-revival mansions built by Abner Cook. Courtesy of Austin-Travis County Collection, Austin Public Library

The Deep Eddy area on the Colorado River has always been a favorite recreation spot for Austin swimmers. In addition to a giant slide, the Deep Eddy swim area had a cable extending out over the water for the more adventurous bathers to swing on. Courtesy of Austin-Travis County Collection, Austin Public Library

Chapter 6

Depression and War: 1929-1945

In 1930, the city's airport was dedicated the Robert Mueller Municipal Airport, in honor of the former city councilman who died in 1926. Courtesy of Austin-Travis County Collection, Austin Public Library

Regular air mail service came to Austin in October of 1930. Courtesy of Austin-Travis County Collection, Austin Public Library

Austin's optimism for the future took a plunge in the fall of 1929. The summer had been exceedingly hot and dry, conditions which not only inflated tempers but also deflated cotton revenues. But problems in Austin were minor in comparison with those of the industrial and financial centers around the country. On October 29, 1929, Black Tuesday arrived, the stock market crash which signalled the end of the old capitalist order in the United States.

The Crash of '29 was received rather calmly in Austin. Since very few Austinites held large fortunes in the stock and bond markets, the crash did not create the psychological trauma experienced in other parts of the country. Most Austin citizens felt secure with the stability of their economy, and very few realized that the crisis facing the industrial cities of the east would affect them.

For over two years the Depression had little effect on the Central Texas economy. Both the state government and the University had embarked on ambitious building programs in 1930 that kept the employment rate high. Business leaders ignored the threat of an impending depression by means of morale-building slogans and confidence-instilling campaigns. But the crisis that had struck the large urban centers had only been delayed, and by 1931 even the most ardent boosters of Austin's economic outlook began to show concern.

Gradually, unemployment figures in Austin rose. Local charities reported that their lists of welfare cases were increasing. The newspaper want-ad columns were full of pleas from individuals searching for work. Farm prices dipped lower and lower. Most oil and mineral production was halted. Industrial and manufacturing plants slowed operations and eventually lay dormant. As a result of this economic stagnation, state revenues dried up, and the state treasury could barely pay its bills. Building activity in Austin tapered off to its lowest level since World War I. When cotton prices reached five cents a pound in 1932 (as compared to eighteen cents a pound in 1928), the Depression had become a reality in Austin. By the summer of 1933, the decline of the Austin economy had reached dangerous levels.

Franklin D. Roosevelt was now in the White House, and a new president had come none too soon for most Austinites. In the election of 1932, FDR carried Travis County by a six-to-one margin. Roosevelt's ability to renew the confidence of a beleaguered people, coupled with revenue and job programs, gave the Texas economy a needed boost. An immediate influx of federal money increased state and university budgets and brought more jobs. The state and university payrolls accounted for nearly one-third of Austin's income. Thus, as their fortunes improved, so did those of the entire community.

When most of the country was falling further into the Depression, Austin could boast of modest prosperity. In 1934, building activity rivaled the mid-twenties boom. The Lower Colorado River Authority was created and began constructing dams along the Colorado. According to longtime resident Walter Long, the sixty-mile network of improvements on the river was "the major factor having to do with the growth of Austin."

New Deal programs contributed significantly to the rapid recovery experienced by Austin and Travis County. In 1935, Public Works Administration crews were at work throughout the city paving streets, building bridges, digging sewers, and creating parks. New Deal funds were also made available to the public school system for remodeling and new construction projects. The Works Progress Administration financed the development and beautification of Waller Creek and the landscaping of area lakes. The most dramatic evidence of a New Deal project was the construction of the University of Texas Tower.

Those hardest hit by the Depression, the elderly, also benefitted from New Deal measures. Statewide relief was directed from the Austin FERA (Federal Emergency Relief Act) office and was aimed at providing immediate help for the aged and for the indigent unemployed. Many Austin residents welcomed the arrival of social security payments after the creation of that agency in 1935. Local farmers also received assistance in the form of crop insurance, government loans, and guaranteed price support. Austin teenagers were put to work by the Civilian Conservation Corps and the National

After extensive renovation, the Majestic Theater was renamed the Paramount. For the next fifty years the Paramount would bring movies, stage productions, and musical concerts to downtown Austin. Ernest Nalle, an Austin banker and businessman, built the Majestic in 1915. Appearing at the theater during its illustrious, sixty-five-year history were such performers as Enrico Caruso, George M. Cohan, Helen Hayes, Houdini, and the Marx Brothers. Courtesy of Austin-Travis County Collection, Austin Public Library

Youth Administration. Truckloads of youngsters left Austin every morning at daybreak to work on one of the LCRA dams or various conservation projects in the hill country.

The population had grown to 74,000 in 1936, and that figure was rising at a steady rate. People knew that the Austin economy was healthy and began pouring into the city at a rate rivaled only by the early seventies. It was generally believed, however, that people moved to Austin, in the words of a city leader, "just because they wanted to live here, not because they were interested in making a fortune."

The next four years saw the city of Austin shift the burden of relief away from the federal government and back to local government and private charity. In fact, the crisis of the thirties helped establish many new local relief agencies in addition to the Community Chest, the Salvation Army, and the Churches' Relief Service.

Social life in the thirties closely resembled the previous decade except for the reappearance of taverns and saloons along Congress and Sixth streets. UT football gained in popularity, with Memorial Stadium filled to capacity every fall Saturday. Barton Springs was still the place to swim and socialize. The creation of Lake Travis gave Austin another beautiful recreation spot. The capital city continued to thrive on political debate, and colorful governors such as Ma Ferguson and W. Lee (Pappy) O'Daniel kept the debate lively.

For the majority of the country, the effects of the Depression still lingered. The New Deal eased the pain, but the cure did not come until World War II rejuvenated the American economy. When the war did arrive, Austinites joined their fellow Texans in record numbers in answering their nation's call. While Texas had only five percent of the population, Texans accounted for eight percent of the armed forces. Austin recruiting stations overflowed in those last days of 1941. Those left in Austin escaped the horror of combat but faced sacrifice and responsibility at home.

Rationing became a way of life during the war years. The major items on the ration list were meat, sugar, gas, and rubber. Residential yards were transformed into victory gardens. Energy conservation was a patriotic issue rather than an economic one. The feelings of solidarity of purpose in Austin reflected the mood of the entire nation.

Texas, because of its climate and vast territory, became the American army's largest training ground. Within sixty miles of Austin were Fort Hood and the numerous military complexes in San Antonio. In 1943, Del Valle Air Field on Austin's southeast edge was renamed Bergstrom Army Airfield, in honor of John Bergstrom. Killed in the Philippines, Bergstrom was Austin's first casualty of World War II. Before the war was over, hundreds of Austin young men joined Bergstrom in that ultimate sacrifice for their country.

The Carl Mayer Jewelry Company has been a successful enterprise since its founding in 1865. This photo of the old Carl Mayer Building was taken in 1931. Courtesy of Austin-Travis County Collection, Austin Public Library

By 1930, the old Millet Opera House had a new look and a new enterprise inside, the Von Boeckmann-Jones Company. Courtesy of Austin-Travis County Collection, Austin Public Library

Downtown shopping in the 1930s always included a stop at Rosner's Department Store, which was located on Congress Avenue between Fifth and Sixth streets in the old Stelfox Building. Courtesy of Austin-Travis County Collection, Austin Public Library

GRADUATING CLASS WOOLDRIDGE SCHOOL FEBRUARY 1933

Photo Ellison

Wooldridge School
graduating class, 1933.
Courtesy of Austin-Travis
County Collection, Austin
Public Library

Groundbreaking ceremonies
for the construction of
Seton Hospital were held in
1931. Father George
Zimmerman is pictured here
turning the first shovel of dirt.
Courtesy of Austin-Travis
County Collection, Austin
Public Library

Gregory Gymnasium was the home of Longhorn basketball for over forty years. Thousands of UT students will also remember it as the site of long registration lines in the sweltering heat of late August. Courtesy of Austin-Travis County Collection, Austin Public Library

This 1934 photo portrays the wedding reception of Chester Koock and Mary Faulk. Austin attorney Henry Faulk is pictured in the center, to the bride's left. The reception was held at the Faulk family home on West Live Oak Street. In 1946, the residence became Green Pastures, to this day one of Austin's finest restaurants. Courtesy of Anne C. McAfee

Every spring at the University, students celebrate Round-Up. This 1934 parade featured the finalists for the Round-Up Sweetheart. Courtesy of Austin-Travis County Collection, Austin Public Library

Photo
ELLISON
"Austin"

The University of Texas Tower and Littlefield Fountain are the two major landmarks on the University campus. The Fountain was erected in 1932 as a tribute to students who served in World War I. The UT Tower was constructed in 1934-35 with state and federal (Public Works Administration) funds. The Tower rises 27 stories and is 307 feet tall. Courtesy of Austin-Travis County Collection, Austin Public Library

The Varsity Theater is still in operation and still appeals primarily to a University audience. Little has changed on the "drag" since the 1930s. Courtesy of Austin-Travis County Collection, Austin Public Library

Political campaigns in Texas have always been colorful. This entertaining young campaigner displays his "Bucking for Ma" vehicle at the Capitol. Ma Ferguson was twice elected governor of Texas. Courtesy of Austin-Travis County Collection, Austin Public Library

As the automobile expanded in popularity, a new term appeared in the American vocabulary, "tourist court." One of Austin's first tourist courts was the Petrified Forest Lodge. When it was constructed in 1934, it was located just north of the city limits. Today it is still standing at 4505 Guadalupe. Courtesy of Austin-Travis County Collection, Austin Public Library

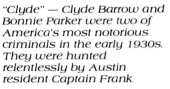

"Clyde" — Clyde Barrow and Bonnie Parker were two of America's most notorious criminals in the early 1930s. They were hunted relentlessly by Austin resident Captain Frank Hamer of the Texas Rangers. Hamer caught the pair in 1934, and they were killed in a gunfight with law officers. Courtesy of Austin-Travis County Collection, Austin Public Library

• "Bonnie" — Although Bonnie and Clyde operated out of Dallas, they went on several crime sprees into Central Texas. Within a three-day period, the notorious couple was credited with a bank robbery in Temple, one in Austin, and two in San Antonio. Courtesy of Austin-Travis County Collection, Austin Public Library

Drought is rare in Central Texas, but this view of the Colorado River reveals the water level at an exceptionally low point. After the elaborate dam system was created along the upper Colorado, high and low water levels could be more accurately controlled. Courtesy of Austin-Travis County Collection, Austin Public Library

The most devastating flood in Austin history occurred in June of 1935. This picture captures the awesome volume of the Colorado River after days of intense rainfall. The water level is just below the Congress Avenue bridge. Courtesy of Austin-Travis County Collection, Austin Public Library

Floodwaters extended several blocks up South Congress, destroying houses, automobiles, and power lines in their path. Courtesy of Austin-Travis County Collection, Austin Public Library

Another view of Congress Avenue demonstrates the power of the floodwater. Asphalt streets were destroyed all along the river. Courtesy of Austin-Travis County Collection, Austin Public Library

One of the most dramatic events during the flood was captured in this photo of a house swept over the dam. Courtesy of Austin-Travis County Collection, Austin Public Library

Following the devastating flood in 1935, local, state and federal officials devised plans to dam up the Colorado River at various spots north of Austin. The Lower Colorado River Authority was created, and work was begun to tame the Colorado. Within a few years, the Highland Lakes emerged from the dam projects and provided power and recreation to thousands of Central Texans. This is an aerial photo of Mansfield Dam, fifteen miles northwest of Austin. Lake Travis is on the left, and Lake Austin is on the right. Courtesy of Austin-Travis County Collection, Austin Public Library

During the Depression, a sale packed the stores with bargain-hunting consumers. In 1935, one could buy a pair of shoes for $2.98, a shirt for 98¢, or a pair of shorts for 15¢. Courtesy of Austin-Travis County Collection, Austin Public Library

When Eleanor Roosevelt
visited Austin in the 1930s,
she met with several of the
city's leading women. Left to
right: Mrs. W.R. Long, Velma
Hunter, Mint Reed, Nina
Bremond, Camille Butler,
Eleanor Roosevelt, Dot
Wilcox, Lutie Perry, and Mrs.
Bickler. Courtesy of Austin-
Travis County Collection,
Austin Public Library

Snow is so rare in Austin
that schools and businesses
usually shut down to
witness the strange weather.
It appears as if that is the
case at the University during
this 1935 snowstorm.
Courtesy of Austin-Travis
County Collection, Austin
Public Library

To restore confidence to the troubled American economy was a major goal of Franklin Roosevelt's New Deal. Billboards similar to this one in downtown Austin were common all over the country: "Prosperity's Rose Blooms Again With Roosevelt." Courtesy of Austin-Travis County Collection, Austin Public Library

One of the Texas governors who faced the trying economic hardships of the Depression years was Governor James Allred. Allred is seen in this photo at the Governor's Mansion trying on a pair of boots to "kick off" the Texas Centennial celebration in 1936. Courtesy of Austin-Travis County Collection, Austin Public Library

President Franklin D. Roosevelt made a campaign swing through Austin in June of 1936. FDR was well-loved in Austin and won all four of his presidential elections in Travis County by healthy margins. Courtesy of Austin-Travis County Collection, Austin Public Library

Austinites celebrated the Texas Centennial in 1936 in a variety of ways. Scarbrough's Department Store displayed their line of Texas-made underwear during "Made in Texas Week." Courtesy of Austin-Travis County Collection, Austin Public Library

Austin in the 1930s was still a relatively small town. This aerial photograph shows how the city concentrated growth and development around downtown, the Capitol, and the University. There is virtually nothing north of the Hyde Park area. Courtesy of Austin-Travis County Collection, Austin Public Library

These men are at work on one of the many city improvement projects sponsored by New Deal agencies. Courtesy of Austin-Travis County Collection, Austin Public Library

The Anderson High School band assembled near Rosewood Park for this 1937 picture. Courtesy of Austin-Travis County Collection, Austin Public Library

Shacks and shanties throughout Austin were evidence of the extreme poverty that the Depression had created. Courtesy of Clarksville Neighborhood Center

This view of South First Street looking to the north was taken in the summer of 1936. The street is being widened and paved for the first time. Courtesy of Austin-Travis County Collection, Austin Public Library

Development in west Austin progressed slowly until the 1940s. This 1937 view of Enfield Road shows it dead-ending at Pecos Street. Courtesy of Austin-Travis County Collection, Austin Public Library

Throughout the 1930s many New Deal projects were in progress at various Austin locations. The widening of the West Twenty-Fourth Street bridge at Lamar is an example of a Public Works Administration effort in 1938. Courtesy of Austin-Travis County Collection, Austin Public Library

Mirror Lake in Zilker Park was built in 1936 with funds and labor provided by New Deal relief programs. Courtesy of Austin-Travis County Collection, Austin Public Library

Hondo Crouch, an All-American swimmer at UT in 1938, "examines" the horses in Littlefield Fountain. Forty years later, Hondo stood as one of the most beloved figures in the folklore of Central Texas.

Hondo was a rancher, poet, and entertainer who exemplified the spirit of the Texas hill country that he loved. He promoted himself as the "Clown Prince of Texas" and as an "Imagineer." In the words of poet Charles John Quarto: "Hondo, he drew a lasso 'round our hearts/ And drew us to his side./ He gave wisdom out like Halloween candy." Courtesy of Becky Crouch Patterson

The Clarksville Colored School, built in 1917, was a one-room schoolhouse that offered classes in grades one through six. At night the school was used for neighborhood meetings or adult education classes. This photo from the 1930s shows an adult class receiving instruction in math. Many of the programs and services provided in the Clarksville community were sponsored by New Deal agencies. Courtesy of Clarksville Neighborhood Center

Streetcar rails were removed from most Austin streets in 1940. In this May 1940 photo, workers are finishing the job on East First Street. Courtesy of Austin-Travis County Collection, Austin Public Library

Visitors from all over the state jammed the Capitol grounds in January of 1941 to witness the second inauguration of W. Lee (Pappy) O'Daniel as governor. Courtesy of Austin-Travis County Collection, Austin Public Library

When Austin turned 100 years old, a parade down Congress Avenue honored the early leaders and settlers who had made it a thriving and prosperous city. Courtesy of Austin-Travis County Collection, Austin Public Library

In 1941 there was little development alongside Lake Austin. This aerial photograph of Tom Miller Dam reveals the beauty of the lake and adjoining hills. Courtesy of Austin-Travis County Collection, Austin Public Library

Downtown Austin, 1943.
Courtesy of Austin-
Travis County Collection,
Austin Public Library

Rarely will Sixth Street
appear deserted as in this
1939 photo. Business and
social activity has always
flourished on Sixth, and a
renaissance of restoration in
the seventies insures that its
attraction will continue.
Courtesy of Austin-Travis
County Collection, Austin
Public Library

The Alamo Hotel at Sixth and Guadalupe has been the residence of many local and state politicians. During the 1930s and 1940s, the tavern on its ground floor was a favorite gathering place for politicians and various local characters. Courtesy of Austin-Travis County Collection, Austin Public Library

Everyone joined in the parade down Congress to celebrate the World War II victory. Courtesy of Austin-Travis County Collection, Austin Public Library

Servicemen stationed at Bergstrom could receive a friendly welcome at the Austin USO Club. Courtesy of Austin-Travis County Collection, Austin Public Library

In August of 1945, Austinites were literally "dancin' in the streets" to celebrate the end of World War II. Courtesy of Austin-Travis County Collection, Austin Public Library

Admiral Chester Nimitz, naval commander of United States forces during World War II, received a hero's welcome on his return to Austin in 1945. Admiral Nimitz's home was Fredericksburg. Courtesy of Austin-Travis County Collection, Austin Public Library

Banquets honoring the returning servicemen were common in the months following the end of the war. The expressions on these faces reflect the mood of the entire country after four long years of conflict. Courtesy of Austin-Travis County Collection, Austin Public Library

Chapter 7
Change and Challenge: 1945 ~ 1981

Children from state institutions and schools have contributed in many ways to the quality of life in Austin. These children from the Texas School for the Blind perform in a play on George Washington's birthday. Courtesy of Austin-Travis County Collection, Austin Public Library

The Texas School for the Deaf has served Austin and the state of Texas since the 1850s. This 1947 photo displays the Victorian Gothic style that characterized the state asylum buildings. Courtesy of Austin-Travis County Collection, Austin Public Library

Change occurred rapidly in Austin after the war ended in 1945. That change was most evident at the University. Thousands of returning veterans chose the University of Texas for their college education, and the University had difficulty successfully assimilating them all. Temporary classrooms were hastily constructed. Barracks and army Quonset huts dotted the campus and lined Lake Austin Boulevard to serve as student housing. More than ever, social and cultural life in Austin revolved around the growing University. Its influence and reputation were spreading, probably because of the eminence of several faculty members rather than its burgeoning physical plant. Men such as J. Frank Dobie, Walter Prescott Webb, and Roy Bedichek gained national fame for themselves and the University of Texas.

The stereotyped generalizations that often describe the fifties in America appear to apply accurately in Austin. Politically, it was an extremely conservative period. The Texas Democratic Party, led by Governors Shivers and Daniel, bore no resemblance to Democrats of the North or West. Political corruption was often the rule rather than the exception. Austin was the storm-center of numerous insurance scandals and bribery allegations. Over 300 indictments were returned as a result of conflict-of-interest violations by state officials and legislators. The conservatism in the political system reflected the conservatism in social relations of the period. Civil rights violations occurred in every segment of society, some even originating from the Governor's Mansion. Austin, as well as most Texas cities, refused to acknowledge the mandate from the Supreme Court to integrate its public schools. When the University of Texas Law School was forced to admit a Black man, the nation witnessed the reluctance of Texas, Austin, and the University to willingly obey the United States Constitution.

Violations of the Constitution were not limited to Texas, however. This was the McCarthy era, the vigilante-style witch-hunt for "subversives" or "common travellers." No one person was victimized more by that dangerous period in our history than one of Austin's own, John Henry Faulk. Faulk, who gained nationwide fame as a humorist and radio personality in the early fifties, was blacklisted for his efforts to challenge the insanity of the McCarthy tactics and constitutional abuses. Eventually vindicated, the celebrity from South Austin emerged as a symbol of the most sacred American tradition: the willingness to fight and sacrifice for the freedoms promised under the Bill of Rights.

With the onset of the sixties, the physical appearance of Austin began to change. New housing developments sprang up in the hills to the northwest. Development along Lake Austin all the way to Lake Travis provided huge profits for its investors, but it also created a potential for environmental disaster in the future. Downtown Austin and the state government complex were both building upward and outward. Beautiful East Avenue, with its hilly terrain and striking landscape, was transformed into Interstate 35, known as the Interregional Highway. The small town atmosphere that had attracted legislators, students, and thousands of Texans through the years was a thing of the past.

The conservative consensus of the fifties was also gone, and no city in

A float showcasing UT athletics prepares for the Round-Up parade in 1948. Courtesy of Austin-Travis County Collection, Austin Public Library

Scenes of the Old West could still be seen in Austin as late as 1947. This deliveryman worked for Rawls Lumber Company. Courtesy of Austin-Travis County Collection, Austin Public Library

Thousands hit the streets to celebrate the 1947 inauguration of newly elected Governor Beauford H. Jester. Courtesy of Austin-Travis County Collection, Austin Public Library

Texas was more visible as a symbol of the turbulent sixties than was Austin. Due primarily to the University, Austin became a pocket of activism and creativity in that era when America experienced profound social change. As one ardent Austin booster exclaimed, "Austin is a shining light at the end of the tunnel of Southern and Texas conservatism." Austinites of all ages were active in "the movement" and were responsible for transforming it into the social awareness of the seventies. Long after the anti-war marches, the Black and Chicano rights protests, and the confrontations with the UT administration were over, citizens of Austin continued to be involved in local as well as national issues. Environmental abuse, the feminist movement, minority rights, historic preservation, and uncontrolled growth became vital concerns affecting the quality of life in Austin.

Change continued to be the by-word throughout the decade of the seventies. Energy costs tripled from 1973 to 1976. Rising utility bills became intertwined with the debate over Austin's participation in a controversial nuclear power project. A new wave of liberal politics surfaced that challenged the old city establishment. Even the physical appearance of downtown underwent sweeping changes as new money began to invest heavily on Sixth Street. Plans for the revitalization of Sixth Street and of Congress Avenue became reality.

The major issue of controversy in the seventies was growth. The population climbed over the 350,000 mark, and the University was bulging with more than 43,000 students. Concerned Austinites started to question the desirability, or even the possibility, of the city's continued expansion. Their concern focused on more than the usual array of problems facing an urban center; it was aimed at protecting the natural beauty and natural resources that have made Austin a unique city. Many Austinites consider the hills west of town, Lake Travis, Lake Austin, and the Barton Creek watershed to be irreplaceable resources that have become vulnerable because of overdevelopment.

Austin's desirability as a place to live and work was well known by the early seventies. An infusion of talented and creative musicians who blended their heritage of rock and folk music with the traditional country sound added to Austin's reputation as one of the social and cultural centers of the southwest. Overnight Austin became the home of "progressive country music." Leaders of that early group were Austin residents Jerry Jeff Walker, Michael Murphey, and Willie Nelson, whose profound effect on the national music industry continues to this day. However, the progressive label soon died out as Austin music diversified and expanded to embrace other musical forms. Today the Austin music scene offers country to jazz and rock to classical. In fact, the Austin Symphony Orchestra has provided the finest in classical music since its inception in 1911.

Even as Austin becomes a major metropolitan area, the Capitol complex and the University seem to dominate the city's personality. Yet an influx of national corporations has provided thousands of new jobs in electronics, computer science, and other high technology business. The resulting population explosion has yet to change Austin's role as the educational and political center of Texas, but pressures are building to transform Austin and to remake it in the image of other high-rise, glass-and-concrete American cities. The challenge of the eighties will be the manner in which the citizens of Austin respond to those pressures. It is hoped that Austin can retain the tradition and the heritage which has evolved over the past 142 years: love and respect for the beauty of Austin and tolerance and pride in the diversity of Austin's people and their beliefs.

The Drake Bridge (South First Street Bridge) was named for former Austin Mayor William Drake. This 1949 picture of the bridge was taken just after its dedication. Courtesy of Austin-Travis County Collection, Austin Public Library

Members of LULAC (League of United Latin American Citizens) were active in the Mexican-American community of Austin. This 1948 photo was taken of the officers of the Austin chapter. Courtesy of Austin-Travis County Collection, Austin Public Library

Every spring the University hosts the Texas Relays. Hundreds of world-class athletes have performed at Memorial Stadium throughout its history. Left to right: Austin, Rockhold, Thomas, Gruneiser, Vickery, Wallender, Fisher, Reeves, Coach Clyde Littlefield. Courtesy of Austin-Travis County Collection, Austin Public Library

Construction began in 1951 to widen East Avenue in order to make a through-highway. By the end of the decade it was known as Interstate 35. This picture depicts the building of the overpass at Nineteenth Street (Martin Luther King Boulevard). Courtesy of Austin-Travis County Collection, Austin Public Library

Concordia Lutheran College became an accredited junior college in 1951. For the previous twenty-five years it had been a high school and boarding school for boys. Courtesy of Austin-Travis County Collection, Austin Public Library

Two of Austin's most distinguished literary figures, historian J. Frank Dobie and folklorist J. Mason Brewer, are present at this 1952 meeting at Huston-Tillotson College. Pictured from left to right are Frank Wardlaw, Dobie, Buck Hood, and Brewer. Courtesy of Austin-Travis County Collection, Austin Public Library

The Texas vs. Texas A&M football game has been a tradition since the turn of the century. This 1952 contest in Memorial Stadium was no exception, as the packed house will attest. Texas won the game, 32 to 12. Courtesy of Austin-Travis County Collection, Austin Public Library

Local media personality Cactus Pryor is being inducted into the Capitol City Sheriff's Posse in this 1954 photo. Courtesy of Austin-Travis County Collection, Austin Public Library

This aerial view of the University was taken in the 1950s. By the mid-'60s the rapid increase in enrollment necessitated an expansion program that would completely transform the physical appearance of the University area. Courtesy of Austin-Travis County Collection, Austin Public Library

Just south of downtown Austin and the river is the Municipal Auditorium. Built in 1958, the auditorium serves as the convention center for the hundreds of organizations and institutions that meet in Austin each year. Courtesy of Austin-Travis County Collection, Austin Public Library

Austin has always been a political city. This 1958 gathering at Lyndon Johnson's Austin home was held in honor of the birthday of former Vice-President John Nance Garner. Left to right: Speaker of the House Sam Rayburn, former President Harry Truman, Garner, and Johnson (at that time majority leader of the United States Senate). Courtesy of Austin-Travis County Collection, Austin Public Library

The late fifties was a period of civil rights activism and protest. The Austin chapter of the NAACP was at the forefront of the movement to achieve equal opportunity and equal rights for all citizens. Marches, sit-ins, and other protests have been characterized in Austin by their emphasis on order and non-violence. This tradition continued into the sixties as seen in this march down Congress Avenue by supporters of the La Raza Unida Party. Courtesy of Austin-Travis County Collection, Austin Public Library

The Lundberg Bakery and Emporium was restored in 1963 by the Heritage Society and the Junior League of Austin. Built in 1876 by the Swedish settler Charles Lundberg, the Old Bakery and Emporium was later bought by the state and housed Austin's Bicentennial Headquarters. In addition to being an information center, today the Old Bakery features hand-crafted gifts and baked goods supplied by Austin senior citizens. Author photo

Immediately after his speech at the Trade Mart in Dallas, President Kennedy was scheduled to fly to Austin for a dinner and reception. The gathering at the Municipal Auditorium on November 22, 1963, never took place. Courtesy of Austin-Travis County Collection, Austin Public Library

The Austin Aqua Festival began in 1962 and has become a major summer attraction in the social life of Austinites. Sponsored by the Chamber of Commerce, Aqua Festival is a ten-day celebration on the shores and in the water of Town Lake. Pictured is a Mexican Night festival. Courtesy of Austin-Travis County Collection, Austin Public Library

John F. Kennedy brought the Democratic presidential campaign to Austin in the fall of 1960. Governor Daniel and security personnel greet Kennedy at the airport before his visit to the Capitol and his motorcade down Congress. Travis County overwhelmingly supported the Kennedy-Johnson ticket in the November election. Courtesy of Barker Texas History Center, University of Texas at Austin

The University Tower and the Capitol no longer dominated the Austin skyline in 1966. Courtesy of Texas Highways

President Johnson and his family returned home to Austin and the Hill Country often during the LBJ administration. This 1967 photo of the nation's first family was taken as they left services at St. David's Episcopal Church. Pictured from left to right are: Luci Johnson, a Secret Service man, Reverend Charles Sumners, President Johnson, Lynda Bird Johnson, Lady Bird Johnson, and Charles Robb. Courtesy of Austin-Travis County Collection, Austin Public Library

Lyndon Baines Johnson Library and Museum.
   The LBJ Presidential Library, opened in 1971, is one of Austin's major tourist attractions and is an important research facility for scholars. Author photo

Student marches and protests became frequent occurrences at the University in the 1960s. Protests were held against the war in Vietnam, against racism at UT, and against the insensitivity of the UT administration. Courtesy of Barker Texas History Center, University of Texas at Austin

Riot police at a "peace march." Courtesy of Barker Texas History Center, University of Texas at Austin

The largest mass demonstration in Austin history took place following the murders of four students at Kent State University in May of 1970. Thousands marched to show their anger and their sorrow and to denounce the American invasion of Cambodia. Courtesy of Barker Texas History Center, University of Texas at Austin

*Celebration at Pease Park.
Courtesy of Austin-Travis
County Collection, Austin
Public Library*

This is the Rio Grande Campus of Austin Community College. ACC, which opened for classes in 1973, now has an enrollment of over 19,000 students. The Rio Grande facility is the former Stephen F. Austin High School building that was constructed in 1916.

Austin Community College, Concordia College, St. Edward's University, Huston-Tillotson College, and the University of Texas all contribute to make Austin the educational center of Texas. Courtesy of Austin-Travis County Collection, Austin Public Library

A high point in the tradition-laden history of University of Texas football came in 1977 when Earl Campbell won the Heisman Trophy. Campbell is congratulated at the awards ceremony by UT coach Fred Akers and by his mother, Ann Campbell.

Campbell came to UT when Darrell Royal was still head coach and athletic director. The glory years of UT football under Royal produced three national championships. Courtesy of University of Texas Sports Information Office

The Bremond Block, a Victorian neighborhood between the 700 and 800 block of Guadalupe and San Antonio, is a designated national historic district. The six houses in the district were built at various times in the nineteenth century by members of the Bremond and Robinson families. This is the John Bremond House at 700 Guadalupe, owned today by the Texas Classroom Teachers Association. Author photo

Nowhere can one find a more scenic or a more tranquil setting than Hamilton's Pool, located west of Austin on Reimers' Ranch. For centuries Hamilton's Pool has served as a refuge to Indians, Conquistadors, and Texans. Courtesy of Austin-Travis County Collection, Austin Public Library

This view of Lake Austin (the Colorado River) is taken from Mount Bonnell. At this point the Colorado River crosses a geological fault known as the Balcones Escarpment, which separates the Texas Hill Country from the blackland prairies to the east. Therefore, the elevation within the city varies from 400 to 900 feet above sea level. The Balcones Fault is a minor crease in the earth's crust, yet it does have some potential for instability. Earthquakes along its perimeter have been reported in Austin in 1852, 1902, and 1931. Author photo

Nude swimming at the "Hippie Hollow" area of Lake Travis is legal and, of course, it is a very popular place during the hot spring and summer months. These Austinites are testing the clean and refreshing Lake Travis waters. Courtesy of Austin-Travis County Collection, Austin Public Library

Barton Springs, 1980. Author photo

Barton Creek is one of Austin's most scenic as well as most environmentally sensitive areas. The 1970's brought development closer and closer to the creek, its watershed, and Barton Springs. Efforts to protect this invaluable area from over-development are underway and must continue for years to come.

Another priceless greenbelt area, just six miles west of the Capitol along Bee Creek, has been protected by neighborhood and city-wide groups. Through public donations the Wild Basin Wilderness was created to leave some 200 acres of west Austin land in its natural state. Courtesy of Austin-Travis County Collection, Austin Public Library

195

The growth of the women's movement in Austin was one of the most important and most visual of social developments in the 1970s. A leading figure in that movement was Austin attorney Sarah Weddington. Weddington has served as a state representative, general counsel of the U.S. Department of Agriculture, and special assistant to President Carter. Feminists, both male and female, look to Weddington for leadership in the local and national political arena. Courtesy of Barker Texas History Center, University of Texas at Austin

The pastor of the Sweethome Baptist Church, Reverend W.B. Southerland, narrates the history of Clarksville in this photo. The children are on a field trip to investigate the traditions and legacies of Austin's Black citizens. Renovation of the Sweethome Church and other Clarksville landmarks is currently in progress. Courtesy of Robyn Turner

Clarksville's central location made it a choice spot for development in the 1970s. Neighborhood associations and public awareness helped preserve the integrity and tradition of Clarksville when it faced unwanted intrusion. Courtesy of Clarksville Neighborhood Center

Much of the "growth controversy" in the seventies revolved around the construction of the Mo-Pac Expressway. Citizens in northwest Austin were concerned about the possible destruction of the serenity and integrity of their neighborhoods. The issue in southwest Austin involved the potential damage that Mo-Pac would inflict on the Barton Creek region. The controversy and the construction continue. This photo depicts the Mo-Pac hike and bike trail as it crosses the Colorado River. Courtesy of Austin-Travis County Collection, Austin Public Library

Symphony Square, located at Eleventh and Red River, houses the offices of the Austin Symphony Orchestra Society. The square consists of the 350-seat Waller Creek Amphitheater and four restored 100-year-old buildings. The dedication of Symphony Square in 1978 culminated the eight year restoration project of the Doyle House, the Hardeman House, the Jeremiah Hamilton Building, and the old New Orleans Club Building. Symphony Square is the only restoration project in the nation to house a symphony orchestra society. Courtesy of the Austin Symphony Orchestra Society

One of the legends of country music is Austin's own Kenneth Threadgill (center). For many years Threadgill had his own honky-tonk on North Lamar that served as a showcase for his unique talent as well as a training ground for young singers. Janis Joplin began her career with Threadgill in the mid-1960s. Accompanying Threadgill in this photo are two other Austin musicians, Alvin Crow (left) and Slappy Gilstrap. Courtesy of Robyn Turner

Zilker Hillside Theater is the site of a variety of free cultural and entertainment activities. Events at Zilker include drama, ballet, and musical concerts. Courtesy of Austin-Travis County Collection, Austin Public Library

"I want to go home to the Armadillo/ Good country music from Amarillo and Abolene,/ The friendliest people and the prettiest women/ You've ever seen." From Gary P. Nunn's London Homesick Blues

The Armadillo World Headquarters, Soap Creek Saloon, Castle Creek, and Texas Opry House were the Austin night spots where "Austin music" began. The musicians during that exciting period in the early and mid-seventies included Doug Sahm, Steven Fromholz, Marcia Ball, Jerry Jeff Walker, Alvin Crow, Gary P. Nunn, Bobby Bridger, Kinky Friedman, Michael Murphey, Willis Alan Ramsey, Rusty Weir, Townes Van Zandt, B. W. Stevenson, and Willie Nelson. Author photo

The "drag vendors" at Twenty-Third and Guadalupe not only sell handmade and personally designed products, but they have become a tourist attraction as well. Nearly every day of the year shoppers can view the finest in arts and crafts and also be entertained by Austin street musicians, jugglers or poets. Due to the growth and popularity of the drag area entrepreneurs, the city formally recognized the businesses and named the location the People's Renaissance Market. Author photo

Austin is populated by many skilled craftsmen and artisans whose products combine personal integrity with quality workmanship. One such craftsman is bootmaker Charlie Dunn, who has been making boots for over seventy years and is still going strong. Entertainers, sports figures, and political leaders from all over the nation wear the trademark of Charlie Dunn on their feet. Courtesy of Robyn Turner

Jerry Jeff Walker (right) is another of Austin's nationally known musicians. Pictured to Walker's right is his friend and cohort Hondo Crouch, the "Mayor of Luckenbach, Texas." Courtesy of Manny Gammage

The talent of Austin's many artists is displayed not only on canvas, but on the streets as well. Wall murals abound throughout the city, reflecting the imagination and the creativity of the citizenry. This mural on the Varsity Theater at Twenty-Fourth and Guadalupe is being painted by Carlos Lowry and his associates. Courtesy of Robyn Turner

One of the world's finest organ builders is longtime Austin resident Otto Hofmann. President of the International Society of Organ Builders, Hofmann is pictured here in his South Austin shop. Although he builds organs primarily in Texas and the Southwest, Hofmann's fame and expertise are known worldwide. Courtesy of Robyn Turner

Willie Nelson has emerged as one of the country's most famous entertainment personalities. Here Willie is performing at his annual Fourth of July picnic, an extravaganza that often attracts as many as 100,000 fans. Courtesy of Rick Henson

Bibliography

Barkley, Mary Starr. *A History of Central Texas.* Austin: Austin Printing Company, 1970.

Barkley, Mary Starr. *History of Travis County and Austin 1839-1899.* Waco, Texas: Texian Press, 1963.

Bateman, Audray, and Hart, Katherine. *Waterloo Scrapbook 1972-1976.* Austin: Friends of the Austin Public Library, 1976.

Brown, Frank. *Annals of Travis County and the City of Austin.* Archives Collection, Barker Texas History Center.

Crosby, Tony. *An Austin Sketchbook.* Austin: The Encino Press, 1978.

Erickson, Virginia, and McBee, Sue Brandt. *Austin: The Past Still Present.* Austin: The Heritage Society of Austin, 1975.

Fehrenbach, T. R. *Lone Star.* New York: The MacMillan Company, 1968.

Frantz, Joe B. *Texas.* New York: W. W. Norton and Company, 1976.

Hart, Katherine. *Austin and Travis County: A Pictorial History 1839-1939.* Austin: The Encino Press, 1975.

Hogan, William R. *The Texas Republic: A Social and Economic History.* Austin: The University of Texas Press, 1969.

Newcomb, W. W., Jr. *The Indians of Texas.* Austin: The University of Texas Press, 1961.

Williamson, Roxanne Kuter. *Austin, Texas: An American Architectural History.* San Antonio: Trinity University Press, 1973.

NEWSPAPERS

Austin American-Statesman
Austin City Gazette
Austin Daily Tribune
Austin Democratic-Statesman
Texas Democrat
Texas Sentinel
Texas Siftings
The Gold Dollar
The Rolling Stone

Index